THE ONLY TRUE GOD

JAMES F. MCGRATH

The Only True God

EARLY CHRISTIAN MONOTHEISM

IN ITS JEWISH CONTEXT

UNIVERSITY OF ILLINOIS PRESS

URBANA AND CHICAGO

⊗ This book is printed on acid-free paper.

Library of Congress Cataloging-in-Publication Data

McGrath, James F. (James Frank), 1972–
The only true God: early Christian monotheism in its
Jewish context / James F. McGrath.
p. cm.
Includes bibliographical references and index.
ISBN 978-0-252-03418-3 (cloth : alk. paper)
1. Monotheism. 2. Church history—Primitive and early
church, ca. 30–600. 3. Christianity and other religions—
Judaism. 4. Judaism—Relations—Christianity. I. Title.
BL221.M43   2009
231.09'015—dc22   2008045106

Contents

Preface

This book is intended as a work of scholarship to advance our understanding of an important aspect of early Jewish and Christian belief, namely, the idea that God is "one." It has nevertheless been my aim throughout the book to make its arguments accessible to those not already familiar with contemporary scholarship on this subject and thus not to presuppose extensive prior knowledge on the part of those first looking into this topic. I hope those reading this book with a strong background in the study of religion or theology will not begrudge the author the fact that he occasionally stops to explain some of the major concepts and debates.

This book has been many years in the making. Its roots go back to my doctoral work on the Gospel of John. In rethinking whether the Christological debates in the Fourth Gospel were about monotheism, I soon realized that it would be necessary to engage in a wider survey of early Jewish and Christian literature if my interpretation of the Gospel of John were to prove convincing. Having now completed a second book, I suspect that much more remains unsaid on these matters than has found its way into either book.

The discussion in chapter 4 of the relationship between Johannine Christianity and Jewish Christianity makes use of material that was published in an article in *Koinonia* journal, and chapter 6, coauthored by Jerry Truex, originally appeared in the *Journal of Biblical Studies*. Full information about both works can be found in the bibliography.

The author would like to thank the library staff at Christian Theological Seminary and the Inter Library Loan staff at Butler University for providing me with access to the books and articles I needed to complete work on this project. I would also like to thank many of the dialogue partners who, over the years, have discussed various aspects of this subject with me in various forums and/or have influenced my thinking on these matters in important ways, especially (but not limited to) Jerry Truex, James Dunn, Loren Stuckenbruck, Marianne Meye Thompson, Larry Hurtado (whose most recent book I have sought to interact with wherever possible, even though this volume was essentially finished when Hurtado's study appeared; I sincerely regret not having had the opportunity to interact with many more of his points in far greater detail, as indeed his extensive study deserves), Richard Bauckham, Alan Segal, Frances Young, and Laurence Kant. It is my hope that, in taking account of the publications, arguments, and observations of these and many other scholars, my own presentation has taken on greater clarity of expression, even if it is still not found to be persuasive by one and all. It goes without saying that any and all flaws readers may find in this book, and any weakness in the arguments put forward, are entirely my responsibility. Furthermore, where at places I have expressed an opinion or interpretation of the evidence differently from that of other scholars working in the same field, it is my sincere hope that this will not be taken as a sign of any lack of appreciation on my part for their work or their arguments. I have come to view the evidence differently than I used to, and differently from how many of my mentors and colleagues view it, but if any of my own arguments are felt to be persuasive, it is only because I have been able to build on a strong foundation laid by those who have worked on this subject before me. It is therefore my hope that the arguments presented in this book will be accepted in a spirit of dialogue leading to further exploration of the subject. I welcome criticisms and corrections, and I anticipate that as a result of this ongoing conversation, my own views will continue to develop and evolve, even as they have done up until now. I also wish to thank the Early Jewish and Christian Mysticism and Hellenistic Judaism sections at the Society of Biblical Literature for allowing me to present a number of these ideas and receive feedback on them at annual meetings. At several points I have covered ground that I had touched on in earlier publications; however, in each case I have sought to rework the material so that it is in a genuinely new form. I wish to thank those journals and publishers who granted me access to a wider forum of interaction even as early as my years as a doctoral student. Most scholars have had the opportunity to write prefaces such as this one and know how difficult it is to name and thank each and every person who has been particularly influential and/or offered helpful criticism and feedback. I thus wish to offer my thanks to everyone who, in his or her own way, to a greater or lesser extent, helped, encouraged, discussed, debated, or in any other way shaped my thinking on this subject and thus contributed to this book. Many thanks also to the Institute for Research and Scholarship at Butler University for providing financial support in the form of a grant that allowed me to devote time unencumbered by other responsibilities to the completion of this project.

Finally, this book is dedicated to my wife Elena and my son Alex. Thank you for being ever supportive of my work on this project.

1 Monotheism and Method: An Introduction to the Study of Early Jewish and Christian Thought about God

If one were to survey the religious ideas that have made the greatest impact on human history, among them would inevitably be included *monotheism*, the idea that there is only one true God. At times, an attempt to propagate exclusive monotheism has divided a people or brought down a ruler; at other times, it has united tribes or peoples who had previously been at war with one another. Monotheism is an idea that has been used to justify one group's dominance over others, and it has been used to emphasize the idea that all are equal as children of one God. Monotheism, it turns out, has been many different things to different people and at different times in history. Yet there can be no denying its impact and thus its importance as a subject of scholarly study.

Monotheism has also been at the focus of numerous debates, in particular between Christian trinitarians on the one hand, and other monotheists, in particular Jews and Muslims, on the other. Questions that tend to be asked in the context of such debates include whether Christians are in fact truly monotheists at all or whether, on closer inspection, they prove to be "tritheists" whose commitment to monotheism is at best questionable. It may be that questions such as these have led the reader to this book. As important as these questions are, however, it was a set of more fundamental historical questions that led to the writing of this volume. That Jews and Christians came to find themselves divided over the understanding of God's oneness is clear, but what is less clear, and unfortunately is often thought to be clearer than it is, is precisely *when* and *how* the "parting of the ways" over this issue came about. Were Jews and Christians always at odds about the notion that God is one? Precisely when and where did Jews and Christians first begin to disagree over the nature of monotheism? The focus of this study is on seeking answers to such questions with respect to the early days of Christianity as viewed in relation to the Jewish religion in the same period. A study of both pre-Christian and later rabbinic Jewish texts, and of various New Testament documents, leads to the conclusion that the split occurred significantly later than the period in which the texts now incorporated in the New Testament were produced.

This book is born out of the current resurgence of interest in what the earliest Jews and Christians believed about God, how it relates to things that early Christians wrote about Jesus, and how their respective beliefs relate to one another. In the first century C.E., when Christianity first appeared, both Jews and Christians could be heard speaking about how "God is one." The emphasis placed on this idea was understood to set their religious convictions apart from those of other contemporaries. It is this distinctive emphasis on God as one that we today are accustomed to call "monotheism." However, the language of "monotheism" (and, for that matter, "polytheism") is modern terminology, not the way people in the ancient world described themselves. For this reason, there is a serious risk that anyone discussing this topic today will impose a preformed definition of monotheism that may well be alien to the texts being studied. To avoid this pitfall, Larry Hurtado has suggested that "first century Jewish monotheism" be defined as the viewpoint of those Jewish authors in this period who consider themselves to be "monotheists," or in other words, devotees of one God alone.[1] I concur that this is the best possible approach if we are to avoid anachronism. Nevertheless, the question of who if anyone in this period considered themselves monotheists, and if so in what sense, is by no means simple. Although it is crucial to allow the texts themselves to define what "monotheism" meant in this period, the relevant texts and their interpretation cannot be easily disentangled from the meaning they, and the ideas expressed in them, came to have in various religious communities in later times.

Why Is It Problematic to Speak about "Monotheism"?

Many readers less familiar with recent scholarly debates on this subject may well take it for granted that early Jews and Christians considered themselves to be monotheists—and may likewise take it for granted that Jews did not consider Christians to be such because of the beliefs they held about Jesus. Whether early Judaism (and thus also Christianity, which was conceived in and born from the womb of first-century Judaism) was genuinely and universally monotheistic in any sense of the word is in fact currently a much-debated subject. For this reason, in the next chapter I shall attempt to assess the character of Jewish devotion to a single God as evidenced in relevant sources from this period in history. But whatever conclusions scholars may reach about the appropriateness of the *terminology* of "monotheism," it remains important to understand as clearly as possible the precise character of early Jewish and Christian devotion to one God alone. This in turn will assist us in determining whether there were different "types of monotheism" in this period, and if so what the relationship was between them.

Thus, while the aim of this book is to illuminate the character of that which is generally designated "early Jewish monotheism" or "early Christian monotheism" in largely *historical* terms, I nonetheless recognize that these phrases already carry numerous overtones and connotations, not to mention the fact that their theological baggage is in all likelihood well over the weight limit for this flight. This field is in desperate need of new terminology that can be used to speak of the beliefs people held in this period without reading back into the ancient world our modern concepts and assumptions. At one point I toyed with the idea of speaking of early Jewish and Christian *theism* rather than *monotheism*. The former term is generally accepted by most Jews and Christians, as well as most philosophers and theologians, as rightly describing both Judaism and Christianity in spite of their rather different understandings of the Godhead. The term has at times also been applied to figures such as Plato who do not deny the existence of "the gods" while speaking regularly of "the god" in the singular. For this reason, I had hoped that perhaps this term might be an alternative to "monotheism," which seems to prejudge the character of early Jewish and Christian belief in advance. However, as it happens, many classicists and scholars of ancient philosophy conclude that Plato ultimately remains a "polytheist," the way he speaks about "God" in the singular notwithstanding. Substituting another existing term for "monotheism" appears not to take us very far toward achieving greater clarity and precision.

Nor will speaking of "monotheisms" in the plural resolve the matter, since the attempt to speak in a similar manner of "Judaisms" and "Christianities" simply shifts the focus from the things that unite various groups to those that distinguish them. It often does so without adequately clarifying the relationship between the diversity that is seen to exist and possible underlying unifying factors that may have led outsiders to regard such groups as nonetheless part of a single group or movement. Thus I will continue to use "monotheism" throughout this book, although it remains my express aim to explore the *character* of the "monotheism" evidenced in various documents and traditions—without becoming entangled in excessively complicated phrases or excessive parentheses and quotation marks. The question of whether this belief in and allegiance to one God has anything in common with monotheism as it is understood in our time shall be left open, at least initially. I hope that in this way I may be freed from having to use cumbersome phrases such as "what Paul believed about the oneness of God." But if we dare to speak of Paul's "monotheism," it is nevertheless essential to recognize that this way of putting things is ours, not his. All of these qualifications, however tedious, must be offered if we are to have any hope of avoiding the imposition of later concepts on these ancient sources when we use terminology that did not exist when they were written.[2]

Someone unaware of the debates that currently occupy scholars in this field could be forgiven for asking why I feel it necessary to qualify to such a great extent what may seem like a rather common and straightforward term. The reason is, quite simply, that what is generally meant by monotheism today is not necessarily precisely what early Jews and Christians believed. Early Jewish texts regularly mention second figures of various sorts, which are depicted as subordinate to God and yet as having common features with God. In fact, belief in such a figure is so nearly omnipresent in the forms of early Judaism known from extant literature that a few scholars have denied that early Judaism should be deemed monotheistic at all.[3] On the other hand, neither these Jewish beliefs nor even those found in the New Testament writings can be said to express the fully developed doctrine of the Trinity current in most branches of Christianity. Scholars of religion often distinguish monotheism from concepts such as *monolatry,* which is the exclusive worship of one God without necessarily denying the existence of others. In order to avoid confusion, and in order to avoid imposing categories alien to (and thus perhaps inappropriate for the study of) these texts, I shall approach the topic by first describing early Jewish belief in God as we find it expressed in the literature of the period.

I shall then go on to relate and compare the forms of monotheism expressed in Christian sources to what we find expressed in Jewish texts, with the hope of illuminating their relationship, their mutual interaction and influence upon one another, and their development. Whether the sort of belief uncovered is most appropriately labeled monotheism, monolatry, polytheism, or something else entirely is a decision best left to the end of the study rather than its beginning—hence my reluctance either to use "monotheism" in anything more than a preliminary fashion in this chapter or to replace it from the outset with another term that might in the end have proved equally anachronistic and problematic. However, this issue is one of terminology. The aim of this study is less one of finding the best designation for the pattern of early Jewish and Christian belief and more one of accurately describing what these groups believed and practiced based on the textual and archaeological evidence they left behind.

Typologies of the Relationship between Early Jewish and Christian Monotheism

Rather than seeking to be comprehensive in mentioning all the views and nuances of the scholars who have addressed this subject, in this section I shall outline the major approaches typical of contemporary scholarship, highlighting potential problems or difficulties where appropriate. By considering these more basic and general questions of method and approach here, it will be possible to avoid repetition and extended excursuses when I examine various Jewish and Christian texts throughout the remaining chapters of the book.

DEVELOPMENTAL THEORIES

One of the most popular theories concerning early Jewish and Christian understandings of God and the relationship between the two is that which proposes *a development on the part of early Christian theology away from its roots in Jewish "monotheism."* In short, this theory posits that a "parting of the ways" took place, one which was perhaps not entirely one-sided but may still be spoken of accurately as a "departure" on the part of Christians from the strict monotheism of the Jewish parent religion.[4]

I shall consider two viewpoints that I have grouped together because of their commonality of approach and method, even though they reach radically different conclusions. Both represent a return to a school of thought that has been called the "history of religions" approach.

Scholars using this approach seek to focus particular attention on the historical processes that lead to developments in religious thought and practice and on the relationship of ideas and beliefs to their surrounding environment and context. For readers less familiar with this approach to the study of early Judaism and Christianity, other terminology could be used that would be equally appropriate. One could speak of the early Jewish and Christian ideas of God as "evolving," and perhaps the metaphor could be extended further to speak of the rise of Christianity as a case of "punctuated equilibrium," where forces internal and/or external brought about significant developments in a relatively short time period. By adopting this terminology from the realm of biology as a metaphor, we could highlight that all the views discussed in this section posit a crucial impetus and driving force within the early Christian movement, which led to significant developments and changes in the view of Jesus which occurred within the span of at most a few generations. For the first group, that impetus is primarily early Christian experience, and it leads to a development *within* the early Jewish-Christian understanding of God. In the second category, we meet with a catalyst from *outside* the early Jewish-Christian movement, which penetrates it and leads it *away from* its Judaic roots.[5]

INITIAL IMPULSE LEADING TO EARLY INNOVATION

Few have done more to revitalize contemporary study of early Jewish monotheism and its relation to early Christianity than Larry Hurtado. Hurtado, as I have noted, advocates a text-focused approach, allowing ancient authors to define what devotion to a single God meant to them. This study seeks to adopt a similar approach, allowing the texts from this period to define for us what monotheism did and did not mean to various individuals and groups whose allegiance to one God alone set them apart from others in their day and age. Hurtado's work on this subject also focuses on the importance of religious experience in the appearance of religious innovations. For Hurtado, the key defining factor in early Jewish monotheism was *worship* or devotional practice.[6] As the first century Jewish author Josephus put it, "The first commandment teaches us that there is but one God, and that we ought to worship only him."[7] It was practices such as sacrifice, offering incense, prayer, and invocation of the name in a sacral context that defined religious allegiance, and it was precisely in these areas that early Christians made innovations that moved them not away from monotheism but toward a different sort of monotheism, one redefined so as to incorporate the exalted status of Jesus.

Hurtado's approach is the one I find extremely helpful, and what disagreements I shall express are an attempt to add nuances to my position vis-à-vis the evidence. For example, I agree with Hurtado about the importance of worship as defining what Jewish allegiance to one God alone meant and how it was recognized. However, there is a need for greater clarity regarding what *type* of worship was the key issue and whether most Jews and Christians would have agreed or disagreed on this particular point. The Greek word for "worship" (*proskynēsis*) could denote a range of practices, from prostration before another individual to animal sacrifice. The practice of the former before figures distinct from God did not always raise controversy in a Jewish context, while the latter pretty much always did. What kind of worship marked the boundary for most or all Jews? How much disagreement was there, if any, over the exact boundary lines? As Hurtado rightly points out, the willingness of Jews in this period to accept martyrdom rather than offer sacrifice to other gods indicates that there was a line that at least some recognized as absolute. However, to assume that the same individuals would have given their lives rather than bow before another human being is unjustified without further investigation.[8]

Esther 3:5, for instance, depicts Mordecai as unwilling to bow before another human being, Haman. Yet it is difficult to know how typical this was of Judaism in the Greco-Roman era, and the exact reasons why Mordecai would not bow before Haman are not explicitly stated. In the Hebrew version of Esther, it could easily be understood that Mordecai did not consider Haman worthy of that sort of honor and respect because of Haman's character rather than because of any particular theological scruples on Mordecai's part. In the additions to Esther in the Apocrypha, 13:12–14, Mordecai is presented as saying he will not bow before any but God. Yet he goes on to say something that is instructive, namely that he would have been willing to kiss the soles of Haman's feet if this would save Israel. However, it is hard to imagine a version of this story, within what we know of Judaism, in which Mordecai had said that he would gladly have bowed to idols or in which he said he would have sacrificed to the emperor if it would have saved Israel. When it comes to such issues, we find far less diversity of viewpoints expressed in Jewish literature and a willingness to kill or die rather than participate in sacrifice offered to anyone other than the one true God.

Hurtado himself draws attention to the breadth of meaning of the word "worship." Yet his attempt to resolve the matter by defining worship in the narrow sense as "treating a figure as divine" could easily become a circular argument.[9] For it is precisely the question of whether early Christians offered to Jesus the kind of worship reserved for one God alone that we need to answer. If prostration before another figure was the key issue in defining monotheism, then the early Christians appear to have departed from Jewish monotheism. However, using the same standard, we would have to conclude that many of their non-Christian Jewish contemporaries had also moved away from strict observance of monotheistic scruples.[10] On the other hand, if animal sacrifice was the key issue, then the failure of Christians to offer such sacrifices to Jesus suggests that the early Christian movement adhered to Jewish monotheism.[11] If the line was drawn somewhere in between, or in different places by different people, then the matter becomes much more complex. Yet even based on the evidence I have mentioned thus far, it seems probable that there were issues that were regarded as unquestionable by most Jews, and others on which a range of opinions existed. There were issues on which it might be possible to compromise, and others for which many if not all would lay down their lives if necessary. Although we have already seen some indication that sacrifice provided the clearest boundary line, and the one on which there was the most universal agreement, we will nevertheless still need to survey the evidence (particularly from archaeology) further in the next chapter.

So while I agree that (to adopt a metaphor that Hurtado himself has used) a "mutation" took place in early Christianity, I feel there is need for greater clarification regarding precisely what was different and whether or not it indeed marked a departure from Jewish monotheism as understood in this period.[12] Elaborating further the evolutionary metaphor, mutations occur in individuals, whereas evolution occurs in species or gene pools. Thus Christianity's "worship" of Jesus is a mutation *within* early Jewish and Christian monotheism. This mutation eventually leads to the production of a new species (trinitarian monotheism), but it is important not to read too much of what happens later back into the earlier period as though a single mutation, however significant, had made the appearance of the new species inevitable. For a new species to appear, a single mutation is not enough. There must also be, among other things, factors in the environment that encourage the mutation to become dominant within a significant segment of the population group. In this book I will argue that although we obviously will eventually end up with two distinct "species" of religion in a later period, they were not yet such in the first century C.E. and monotheism was not yet one of the issues around which the divergence toward speciation centered.

INFLUX OF GENTILES LEADS TO
BELIEF IN JESUS AS A SECOND GOD

Taking up the argument of an earlier generation of scholars, Maurice Casey has argued that as Christianity became increasingly less Jewish, so too it became increasingly less monotheistic.[13] As I and others have argued elsewhere, this approach fails to do justice both to the Jewish self-understanding of the earliest Christians (who make exalted claims about Jesus) and to the close parallels that can be found to early Christological language in Jewish literature from the same period. The same problem that is seen from our standpoint in history regarding whether the early Christians were monotheists has been raised in relation to the Judaism of the same time period. There is nothing within Christianity's doctrine of God in the very earliest period that could not have been taken over from Judaism, nothing that requires us to posit the influence of non-Jewish ideas of God within the early Christian community. Indeed, the early Christians continued to distinguish themselves from their wider Roman context in the same ways that Jews did, for example, by refusing to offer sacrifice to the Roman gods or the emperor. They remained firm on this, for the most part, in spite of the obvious cost, and this makes the attempt to attribute the Christian doctrine of God primarily to the influence of this wider Roman context highly implausible.

Recent scholarship on early Judaism has focused a great deal of attention on the existence of various intermediary figures, such as angels and personified divine attributes, and the exalted role attributed to human figures such as Enoch, Moses, and Abel. It is thus quite possible that early Christianity's view of Jesus, even the more developed Christology of John's Gospel and later theologians, may owe more to Christianity's Jewish roots than the model of "the parting of the ways" indicates. However, there are many different views regarding how to interpret this evidence, so no conclusions can be drawn until we have engaged in a more detailed analysis of some of the relevant texts. Even at this stage, however, it is worth drawing attention to the lack of debates specifically about "monotheism" in the New Testament or even in the earliest church fathers. As I shall argue in greater detail later, the focus of disagreement between Jews and Christians in the literature of at least the first two centuries of the Christian era was not about the conviction that God is one. Rather, this appears to be a belief that both sides took for granted.

Nevertheless, there are exceptions to this general statement, and thus we find on the Christian side groups such as the Gnostics, who did not find a multiplicity of divine beings or emanations problematic when other Christians did, while on the Jewish side we have those intriguing rabbinic polemics against people who believed there are "two powers" in heaven. More shall be said on these points in subsequent chapters. At this stage, it is sufficient to indicate that the "parting of the ways" model of the relationship between Jewish and Christian views of God may prove to be, at best, oversimplified. With the idea of God as one being axiomatic among both early Jews and Christians, and recognized as such by those both within and outside these religious communities, it is hard to imagine that a group could simply "drift away" from monotheism. If there was a departure from monotheism, then some explanatory mechanism must be found. If there was in fact no departure from monotheism on the part of the earliest Christians, then one still needs an explanation of how Jews and Christians came to disagree over the doctrine of God over the course of the centuries that followed. That a parting of the ways took place is clear. It remains a distinct possibility, however, that the idea of God's oneness was not initially an issue that contributed to the rupture.

STATIC THEORIES

While some are persuaded that the early Christians departed from strict Jewish "monotheism," others have suggested that neither early Jews nor early Christians were truly "monotheists." In other words, this approach claims that there is a fundamental agreement between their doctrines of God, none of which are truly monotheistic.[14] Although I shall attempt to determine the character of Jewish belief in the Greco-Roman period in the next chapter, unfortunately I shall not be able, in the context of this study, to investigate the separate question of exactly *when* Judaism (or the religion of ancient Israel) became monotheistic in any sense. Some recent scholarship suggests that the rhetoric of monotheism found in writings like Deuteronomy in fact attempts to obscure, and at the same time transform, an essentially nonmonotheistic belief system that existed in the pre-exilic era. However, if by the Roman era most or all Jews considered it appropriate to worship only Yahweh and him alone, then the fact that some or perhaps even all earlier Israelites were "polytheists" is to a large extent irrelevant for our understanding of Jewish thought, belief, and practice in the period in question. Granted, if the figure of Wisdom (to take but one example) has its roots in an earlier Israelite goddess, then an understanding of this development may explain some of the features attributed to Wisdom by Jewish authors. However, to whatever extent such origins of the figure seem to be repudiated or ignored, at least on a theoretical level, by authors of this period, then we may be justified in adopting an essentially *synchronic* rather than a *diachronic* approach.

The writings of the Deuteronomistic school clearly seek to create and enforce a "monotheistic" and aniconic approach to the worship of God. The only question that is directly relevant to the subject addressed in this book is how quickly they succeeded in winning most or all of those who considered themselves Jewish in this period to their vision of Judaism and whether at least the great majority of those who considered themselves Jewish in the Greco-Roman era adhered to this view of God. Neither the existence of Deuteronomy nor its wide dissemination among Jews will answer our question, since even in our era of literacy the existence of the printed Bible and its acceptance in Christian communities are hardly sufficient evidence to decide whether all, some, or anyone at all among them adheres to particular ideas or practices found therein. The relevant evidence for our purposes is the evidence regarding how Jewish individuals and communities *interpreted*, or perhaps *ignored*, these texts and applied or failed to apply them in their lives.

One other not dissimilar viewpoint that ought to be mentioned under this heading is that of John O'Neill. As far as O'Neill is concerned, both early Jews and early Christians were essentially trinitarian in their belief concerning God, so that Christians did not depart from the Jewish beliefs they already held. This is perhaps the most unusual of all the theories, and O'Neill appears to be its only proponent (although there are noticeable similarities with both the position of scholars such as Margaret Barker and Peter Hayman on the one hand and the position put forward recently by Richard Bauckham on the other).[15] The fundamental problem with O'Neill's approach is that it attributes to Jewish authors doctrines that most scholars would agree were not even held by Christians yet. In the texts of this period (including many early Christian ones), designations like "Word," "Wisdom," and "Spirit" seem to refer interchangeably to the same reality. Thus at most it might be possible that Judaism held to some form of "binitarianism." But whereas later trinitarianism developed highly technical terminology to refer to the members of the Godhead (terms such as "person" or "hypostasis"), in Jewish texts from this period we are never quite certain that these are not simply highly developed metaphors and personifications. Even in the New Testament, it is not entirely clear when some of the language used in relation to Jesus is literal and when it is not. In both cases, however, we find language used that implies continuity with God and also language that implies separateness and subordination. The meaning of such language has been debated for centuries, and a book of this length is unlikely to settle these matters definitively. What is important at this stage is that those areas where matters are uncertain be highlighted. O'Neill's interpretation shows that it is possible to read not only Christian texts, but early Jewish ones as well, as reflecting a form of trinitarian belief. Even if he is mistaken, he has helpfully highlighted the similarities between the language used in early Judaism and Christianity, and any interpretation of the evidence must do justice to this point. At any rate, the question of whether it is appropriate to call early Judaism trinitarian is much like the question of whether it is appropriate to call Judaism and Christianity monotheistic. It all depends how one defines the term in question.

It should be clear from the preceding discussion that the monotheism of the Judaism of this period may have been far more flexible than previous generations of scholars recognized. A helpful attempt to do justice to this fact has been made by Richard Bauckham, who seeks to introduce clarity into our understanding of Israel's concept of the uniqueness of its one God. He makes use of the concept of *divine identity* in an attempt to get beyond traditional distinctions, which understood God's uniqueness functionally (i.e., in terms of his unique activity), liturgically (i.e., in terms of the dividing line provided by cultic worship), and/or ontologically (i.e., in terms of his nature). For Bauckham, God's unique identity relates to four key points:

1. God has a name, Yahweh, setting him apart from all other gods.
2. Yahweh is the God who brought Israel out of Egypt.
3. Yahweh is the sole creator of all things.
4. Yahweh is the sovereign ruler of all things.[16]

My hesitation to agree with Bauckham results from the fact that three of the four identifying characteristics are plagued by a far greater degree of ambiguity than Bauckham acknowledges. That Israel's God alone had been involved in bringing the nation out of Egypt was not significantly disputed, although the possibility that theophanic manifestations of God might be mediated through angelic presences is not explicitly addressed in the literature of this period, in the way that it is in the Passover Haggadah in the form it is known today (see, e.g., Numbers 20:16). Be that as it may, there is evidence for God sharing not only his role as creator and his sovereignty, but even his *name* with one or more other figures. This is not to say that the one God did not consistently maintain a priority of some sort over the figures in question. But this issue remains crucial for the understanding and demarcation of those highly elusive "dividing lines" of Jewish belief in one God. In fact, given that even the divine name could be shared so as to empower an angelic figure with God's authority, it is appropriate to ask whether Judaism in this period thought in terms of a "dividing line" at all, or whether it understood the uniqueness of their own "God Most High" in some other way.

Bauckham maintains that the Jews had a clear understanding of God's unique identity and nature. In his own words, Israel understood its God to be "not merely at the summit of a hierarchy of divinity, but in an absolutely unique category, beyond comparison with anything else."[17] The dichotomy presupposed here, as I will argue in greater detail, is a false one. Israel's God may well have been in the unique, incomparable position of being at the summit of the hierarchy not just of divinity but of all being. Yet in terms of the dividing line of *creation*, it simply does inadequate justice to the literary evidence to demand that there be no "blurriness" whatsoever as to whether a figure was intrinsic to the divine identity or separate and subordinate thereto. No text makes this point more clearly than Philo's statement in *Who Is the Heir of Divine Things?* (206).[18] There the Word (Greek *Logos*) is described as "neither uncreated as God, nor created . . . but between the two extremities." Indeed, a greater degree of blurriness seems hard to imagine, especially in relation to a "figure" that sometimes appears to be none other than God himself yet at other times is depicted as separate, subordinate, and inferior. The phrase "neither uncreated nor created" suggests that whereas there was a clear difference or distinction posited between Israel's God as the source of all things on the one hand and his creation on the other, the boundary may well have been more like a river than a wall. In other words, like a river that marks a country's border, the existence of a border, indeed its general location, may be clear, and nevertheless the edges of that border may be quite literally "fluid." It is thus possible that Jews, like others in this period, believed that the highest God created all things and was the source of a hierarchy of being which has its origins in him and which proceeds from him through the Logos, angels, humans, and various other forms of life and existence.[19] If this is the case, then the distinctiveness of Israel's God, and Israel's distinctive allegiance to this one God, shall need to be defined in other terms.

Similarly, in the case of divine sovereignty, it does not appear that the exercise of divine power placed one firmly on the divine side of the supposed "gap" between Creator and creation. In fact, as numerous studies of the concept of *agency* in Judaism have shown, God is regularly depicted as sharing his sovereignty with an appointed agent. For the benefit of readers who may not have encountered the term "divine agent" as used in biblical scholarship, it should be mentioned that it is not referring to individuals who sold houses for God or booked gigs for God to perform at local clubs on Saturday nights. When we speak of "agency" we are speaking of what in Greek would have been called "apostleship"—the situation in which someone is sent to represent someone else. In the days before mobile phones, fax machines, the Internet, and telecommunications, this was an essential aspect of communication and interaction with others. If a king wanted to make peace (or war) with another nation, he did not go in person—or at least not in the first instance—but sent his ambassador. When a wealthy person wanted to arrange a property purchase or sale in another region, he sent a representative. When God wanted to address his people, he sent a prophet or an angel. Agency was an important part of everyday life in the ancient world. Individuals such as the prophets and angels mentioned in the Jewish Scriptures were thought of as "agents" of God. And the key idea regarding agency in the ancient world appears to be summarized in the phrase from rabbinic literature so often quoted in these contexts: "The one sent is like the one who sent him."[20] The result is that the agent can not only carry out divine functions but also be depicted in divine language, sit on God's throne or alongside God, and even bear the divine name. Further discussion of the evidence will be presented in later chapters as we compare such concepts and motifs in Jewish literature with the way the earliest Christians wrote about Jesus. For the present, we may simply draw attention to the implausibility of the suggestion that Jews would have held to a theoretical concept of divine identity and uniqueness such as that posited by Bauckham yet have gone on to obscure the clarity of this definition so thoroughly in their writings. In short, if Bauckham's concept of the distinction between God and others in terms of divine identity was the dividing line in this period, then we would have to conclude that there was in fact no dividing line, that there was nothing that set God apart completely and unambiguously from all other figures. However, as we shall see below, there may indeed have been other ways of defining God's uniqueness in this period.

One of Bauckham's strongest points is his willingness to challenge long-standing presuppositions. And thus I wholeheartedly agree with him when he writes, "That Jewish monotheism and high Christology were in some way in tension is one of the prevalent illusions in this field that we must allow the texts to dispel."[21] However, my agreement with this point results from a rather different interpretation of the evidence, as I shall explain in the chapters that follow. To summarize, then, my disagreement with Bauckham does not have to do with the breadth that he allows to the notion of "divine identity" in the Judaism and Christianity of this period. Where I disagree is in relation to his suggestion that the inclusion of Jesus "within the divine identity" genuinely serves as a way of clarifying the development of Christology. To deny that figures from Jewish literature such as the angel Yahoel are genuine parallels and precedents to the claims early Christians made regarding Jesus is at best problematic. In other words, my disagreement with both O'Neill and Bauckham has to do with their depiction of Jewish beliefs in this period, not with their affirmation (with which I agree) that earliest Christianity did not in fact depart from Jewish adherence to one God alone.

Important Scales and Distinctions

In short, then, there have been a number of attempts to relate early Jewish and Christian ideas about God to one another. None of them is entirely without difficulty, but the one that seems most promising emphasizes that the early Christian view of Jesus represented an adaptation within Judeo-Christian monotheism rather than a departure from it. In order to do justice to the evidence without imposing potentially inappropriate categories or dichotomies, it will be helpful to identify explicitly the existence of a range of possible views on a number of crucial issues, which may be outlined briefly in terms of a series of continua.

No development → insignificant elaboration → development

The first way in which different views may be categorized is according to the *degree of development* that is posited between Judaism and Christianity as regards their doctrines of God. Views range from those that deny any distinction to those that insist on a radical distinction, between which are those who discern a greater or lesser degree of elaboration or development.

Sufficient precedent → insufficient precedent → minimal precedent → no precedent

Second, views may be distinguished in terms of the *degree of precedent* that they consider to have already existed within Jewish monotheism.

On the one hand, some believe that the language applied to Jesus by the first Christians was taken over from Judaism and involved no real original contribution on their part. On the other hand, there are some who regard the Christian form of Christological belief as something unique (or at least distinctive) that appeared without any real precedent existing in Judaism. In between, there are various views acknowledging that the early Christians portrayed Jesus and God in terms taken over from Judaism, but without these precedents being able to offer a complete, comprehensive explanation of what was affirmed by the first Christians and why.

> Strictly enforced orthodoxy ➔ unwritten (but accepted) orthodoxy ➔ limited pluralism ➔ pluralism

Third, the views that are held and the conclusions drawn depend to a large extent on one's view of Judaism during this period. While it has become largely accepted that there was no universally enforced Jewish orthodoxy at this time, this does not exclude the possibility that all Jews held to a single traditional view, one that was universally accepted and thus a sort of "unwritten orthodoxy." Others may conclude that there were very different "Judaisms" existing in this period, which opens the door to the possibility that some were more monotheistic than others, and even that some were not monotheistic in any sense at all.

> Metaphorical ➔ hypostasis ➔ separate divine entity

Fourth, as I have noted, numerous Jewish texts allow for the existence of a "second figure" alongside God—of high rank and at times almost blending into God, yet at other times clearly subordinate and distinct. The extent to which one believes that such figures were thought to be real entities or metaphorical personifications will inevitably affect one's view of the relationship between the various Jewish and Christians views of God that existed during this period.

Types of Monotheism

In addition to the importance of distinguishing possible understandings of the relationship(s) between early Jewish and Christian monotheism, it is also important to note the "types of monotheism" that have been and can be identified and distinguished as existing during this period.[22]

RHETORICAL MONOTHEISM

Greek-speaking Jews made use of the slogan *heis theos*, "God is one." This is a phrase that also appears in non-Jewish writings. Yet in some way or other, the Jewish authors who used it appear to have understood it to express something that distinguished Jews from all others and set apart their one God and their belief in him from all others. Rhetorical monotheism is thus, in one sense, not something that is an exclusively Jewish linguistic phenomenon. Rhetorical monotheism has no distinguishing content unless one can discern the dividing lines and make-or-break issues that lie behind and uphold the use of such language. In view of the way Jews made "one God" a focal point of their distinctive identity, it seems inconceivable that there should be no such dividing lines. And yet, as scholarship has clearly demonstrated, recognizing those dividing lines is no easy task. Thus since I agree with Hurtado in accepting texts that affirm monotheism as evidence of the character of first-century Jewish monotheism, I must now proceed beyond this starting point to attempt to find out what distinctive beliefs and/or practices lie behind the Jewish use of the rhetoric of monotheism. It was not the language of "one God" that set Jews apart but the use of this language to summarize other distinguishing beliefs and/or practices that we still need to identify.

CREATIONAL MONOTHEISM

Although we have seen that there are certain problems with the attempt to regard the doctrine of creation as the dividing line between Israel's one God and all other figures, this does not negate the fact that Israel understood its God as the source of all other existing things, however that may be defined. Even the Logos and Wisdom, who stood on the border, could be said to have their ultimate origin with or within God. Nevertheless, it will be useful to respond in this context to certain points made recently by N. T. Wright on this topic.

Wright considers the creational character of Jewish monotheism to rule out certain other types of belief. With regard to only one point do I wish to shade my own position differently than Wright shades his. Regarding his statements that Israel's creational monotheism excludes pantheism, deism, and Gnosticism, I have no quarrel whatsoever. It seems certain that most Jews regarded God Most High as personal and as the good creator of the universe, which excludes pantheism and Gnosticism. Although creational monotheism in itself does not exclude

deism, Israel's belief that the Creator had entered into a special relationship with it and acted on its behalf is obviously something other
than deism. The only question is whether creational monotheism excludes henotheism a priori. Wright, while recognizing that Israel may
have been henotheistic at some point in its history, nonetheless asserts
that "Israel was committed to seeing her god as ontologically (and not
merely practically) superior to the gods of the nations. . . . The gods of
the nations are not 'real' gods; they are idols."[23] This statement seems
to us too sweeping and too simplistic. The Creator, simply by virtue of
being above all else and the source of all other existing things, clearly
has an "ontological" distinctness of some sort. Nevertheless, we ought
not to jump too quickly to the conclusion that Israel had a clear concept of its God as possessing a unique "nature" or "essence." In more
practical terms, it is unjustified to dismiss the possibility that many or
even most Jews accepted the "reality" of other gods. These were clearly
subordinate to the Creator, but this does not mean they were unreal.
In fact, it is quite common for Jewish texts from this period to refer to
"gods" (Hebrew *elohim*) in the plural, a category that included both
gods of the nations and what today we might group under the separate
heading of "angels." These entities, further down the hierarchy of being, were created by and dependent on the Creator. To what extent Jews
would have spoken about a difference of *nature* in a philosophical or ontological sense requires further discussion. What should be clear is that
creational monotheism attributes an ontological *priority* to the Creator
God, but not necessarily an absolute ontological "uniqueness," at least
in the sense that later theology would come to define it.[24]

LITURGICAL MONOLATRY/MONOTHEISM

Many peoples in the ancient world worshipped both a high god and
many others. Israel, it is generally thought, worshipped only the high
God.[25] It has thus been suggested that worship was the key dividing line
between Israel's one God and all others. However, certain ambiguities
in the literary evidence have raised a number of doubts and objections
regarding this approach.

First, "worship" is a broad term and there has been a great deal of
ambiguity in its usage. In reference to prostration before another figure, the evidence seems to clearly indicate that this was not something
reserved for the one God alone. It is true that two Jewish texts (Philo,
*Legatio ad Gaium*116 and Esther LXX 13:12–14) express reservations
about the practice of prostrating oneself before a human ruler.[26] Likewise, several texts express a similar reserve regarding human prostra-

tion before angels.[27] However, on the whole the practice of prostrating oneself before a ruler or other exalted figure appears to be accepted in the Jewish Scriptures and continued into early Judaism. Objections only appear to arise in the case of (1) pagan rulers, whose rule might be regarded as opposed to that of the one God, and (2) angelic figures. The latter cases may be due to two considerations: It is often argued in Jewish writings that the status of angels is not above that of human beings, and there is also the danger of mistaking the angelic messenger for God himself. In neither of these two cases does there appear to be any grounds for assuming that a ban was being placed on prostration before absolutely any figure, especially one who rules on God's behalf as God's appointed viceroy.

An interesting passage that illustrates this point and at the same time suggests a way forward is 1 Chronicles 29:20–23. Here we see the people "worship" (i.e., bow before) Yahweh and the king, with a single verb being used to describe the action addressed to both. Slightly later, Solomon is said to sit upon the throne of Yahweh. Clearly, neither the throne nor the prostration is felt to be problematic by this author. This evidence is important in evaluating the significance of the witness of such writings as the *Exagogē* of Ezekiel the Tragedian or 1 Enoch, with their portraits of prostration before a human figure seated on a heavenly throne. If there is a cultic activity addressed to Yahweh alone, it is sacrificial worship, that is, the slaughter and offering of animals to him (1 Chron. 29:21). Interestingly, even much later, not only Jews but even Christians felt that the offering of animal sacrifices was a make-or-break issue of their fidelity to God, even when they no longer worshipped their own God through such animal sacrifices. Here, it would seem, we have a clear boundary line for most Jews. There is one God, and only one temple, where sacrifices are offered to him and to no other.[28] However, even if this was indeed the definitive boundary marker, there are still questions to be answered. As there was apparently no sacrificial worship of Jesus by the early Christians, does this clarify his relation to Israel's one God? And what of figures that seem to blend "ontologically" into the one God, such as Wisdom and Logos? It seems that this dividing line, while fairly clear, is one of *practice*. Whether a clear *theory* or doctrine underpinned this practice remains to be seen.

INCLUSIVE OR EXCLUSIVE MONOTHEISM?

Relevant to any study of early Jewish and Christian monotheism is the question of self-understanding in relation to others. We have already looked at some possible boundary lines that may have been drawn and used in the process of self-definition. But we must also take into account the possibility of *unconscious influence*. It is possible for a religious group to adopt an ultraconservative or fundamentalist stance on some issue or other, without realizing the extent to which it has nevertheless been influenced by the culture, mindset, or philosophy it claims to oppose. We must thus raise the issue of to what extent Jews were willing to consciously identify their God with those of other nations and the extent to which the influence of other concepts of God consciously or unconsciously influenced early Jewish and Christian forms of monotheism. The issue here is thus not only that of influence but also that of an exclusive or inclusive understanding of the identity of the one God.

The work of E. R. Goodenough has draw attention to the portrayal of Biblical narratives in connection with pagan imagery in the synagogue at Dura-Europos.[29] In this synagogue (built around the middle of the third century CE) one finds not just the zodiacal imagery that is so widespread during this whole period but also depictions of the god Ares supervising the Exodus from Egypt and the three Nymphs guarding the infant Moses. Nevertheless, there is no evidence that these pagan deities and mythical figures were worshipped, whether sacrificially or in some broader sense.[30] This is more a case of the uniting of Israel's sacred narratives with those of the wider Greco-Roman world. However, the (admittedly apparently isolated) case of two individuals who were either Jewish or of Jewish descent leaving an inscription thanking "the god" in a temple of Pan indicates that, for at least some Jews, the view was accepted that the various divine names and concepts of deity ultimately referred to the same being.[31] There was presumably at least a small minority within Judaism who could accept that, in offering worship to Pan, one could in fact offer worship to Yahweh, Israel's God. Pan, after all, means "all" or "everything" in Greek, facilitating the understanding of this god as the universal deity. But that there were such individuals has never been particularly surprising or controversial. The real issue continues to be whether such people were far beyond the pale as far as most Jews in their time were concerned. In the next chapter we will look at a slightly earlier period in Jewish history and see what can be discerned about Judaism's development in the Hellenistic age. Jewish authors of the Roman era are adamant about this subject when they address it, and popular sentiment about issues like the introduction of Roman statues into the Jewish temple in Jerusalem gives a reasonable indication regarding certain key aspects of Jewish belief in this period. Nevertheless, it is important to look earlier and later, and at archaeological as well as textual evidence, to get a clearer sense of just how widespread certain views on this subject actually were.

Also of key importance to this study are the "mediator figures," whether divine, angelic, or human, which appear as a regular feature in Jewish literature during this period. Bauckham claims that "intermediary figures who may or may not participate in divinity are by no means characteristic of the literature of Second Temple Judaism" and for this reason discounts their importance in attempting to understand early Jewish monotheism and early Christology.[32] In my view, nothing could be further from the truth. It is far easier to think of examples of literature from the Second Temple period that contain such figures than of examples that do not. And so it is important to assert from the outset our conviction that it is only by carefully comparing the types of language and attributes attributed to Jesus in the New Testament with similar language applied to other figures in Jewish literature that one can determine what, if anything, is unique in one or the other.

Summary

In this chapter we have seen that there is fundamental disagreement among scholars about whether early Judaism was monotheistic and whether early Christianity marked a departure from Jewish monotheism. With some danger of oversimplification, it might be said that there are three major types of interpretation of the evidence: (1) Both early Judaism and Christianity were monotheistic; (2) neither early Judaism nor early Christianity was monotheistic; and (3) early Judaism was monotheistic and early Christianity departed from its Jewish monotheistic roots. As we shall see in the chapters that follow, early Christian authors do not engage in debates about whether God is one, and they often cite the oneness of God as a presupposition. In deciding which of these options best fits characterizes the evidence, everything revolves around the question of how one defines monotheism and whether it is an appropriate term to use in relation to the beliefs of Jews and Christians in this period.

In order to decide the matter, we shall focus our attention on the evidence from Judaism primarily in the Hellenistic age. When we get into the Roman era, it is clear that there are some vocal spokespersons for Judaism who use the language of one God. This does not prevent some scholars from maintaining that these voices represented a minority viewpoint. It thus becomes important to look back earlier and to assess the extent to which something that may be called "monotheism" appears to have been present in the previous era and how typical it appears to have been. That the religion of ancient Israel during most of the pre-exilic period tended to be polytheistic is widely accepted. That monotheism becomes an appropriate term later on is also largely undisputed. The issue for our purposes is whether this represented the popular, majority viewpoint in the period of the New Testament, and in order to assess this, we need to examine the evidence prior to the time of the birth of Christianity as well. Much emphasis has also been placed on the importance of material remains and archaeological evidence as giving voice to popular belief and practice, over against the evidence of texts, which represent the views of the literate elite minority. We shall attempt to take into account all relevant types of evidence and, most important, the perception of outsiders regarding what was typical of Judaism in this period. By doing so, we can get a glimpse of what Jewish belief and worship looked like in this period and what kinds of "worship" were offered and to whom. It is to these matters that we turn our attention in the next chapter.

2 Worship and the Question of Jewish Monotheism in the Greco-Roman Era

Before we can determine whether various early Christian writings fit within Jewish monotheism as it was understood and practiced in the Greco-Roman period, we must determine whether and to what extent Judaism was in fact a monotheistic faith, and whether there was a unity or diversity of views on the matter. Rather than simply move directly into the evidence regarding the Roman era, it is crucial that we begin earlier, with a review of the evidence that Judaism was recognized by others in the Hellenistic age as having some sort of distinctive focus on one God alone. Because scholars such as Margaret Barker claim that Christianity simply took up elements of a "polytheistic" form of religion that never died out in Israel, it is important to determine the character of Jewish beliefs not only in New Testament times but also for several generations before. Then and only then will we be in a position to explore possible categories of classification that may enable us to do justice to both Jewish distinctiveness, as well as to the fact that this distinctive focus on one God may not be identical to what is generally meant by terms such as "monotheism" in our time.

There are three major possibilities when thinking about Jewish monotheism and/or polytheism in this period:

1. It is possible that "in those days there were no rules in Israel, and everyone did as he saw fit." In other words, the diversity within Judaism may have included both what we might call monotheists (or perhaps "Yahweh-aloneists") and polytheists. Within this latter category might be included both those who continued a pre-exilic form of religion that remained uninfluenced by the Deuteronomic innovations of the reign of Josiah, such as appears to have existed at Elephantine in Egypt, and those who engaged in worship of the local gods in those parts of the Diaspora where they lived.[1] According to this view, there is simply a diversity of "Judaisms," of groups who may well have had nothing in common apart from their bearing of the designation *Ioudaioi*, "Jews."

2. It is possible that there were rules that most if not all Jews considered binding and authoritative, such as for example those found in the Torah. If this was the case, then as scholars for such a long time maintained, things like the inscriptions to Pan made by Jews living in the Diaspora were exceptions, ones that would have presumably been considered by most Jews to be beyond the pale of acceptable practice. When I say there may have been rules, I do not mean this in the sense of a universal orthodoxy, which clearly did not exist in this period. What I mean is that the view that one should worship only one God could by this stage in their history have become a well-established part of Jewish identity, self-understanding, and culture. There are plenty of viewpoints that can be regarded as the opinion of the majority of Americans in our time but two hundred years ago were completely unknown.[2] Whether a viewpoint was established by propaganda or by force at some time in the past, or through some slower process of cultural development, matters little. It did not take more than a couple of centuries for Islam to come to dominate in Arabia—or for Protestantism to become the dominant force in certain European countries after the Reformation. Enough time had passed between the origins of the Yahweh-alone movement and the start of the Hellenistic age that, even without some central authority to impose its viewpoint as orthodoxy, this viewpoint could nonetheless have established itself as "common Judaism." Whether it had in fact done so is a matter that must be considered carefully, but it is certainly a genuine possibility and should not be excluded simply because it was assumed without question to be the case by earlier generations of scholars.

3. It is possible that there were rules or a generally accepted viewpoint but that some of the things usually felt by scholars to be examples of "polytheism" or syncretism may in fact have been compatible with devotion to one God alone as understood in Hellenistic Judaism. Paula Fredriksen has said, "While not every ancient polytheist was a monotheist, all ancient monotheists were, by our measure, polytheists."[3] Terms such as "monotheism" and "polytheism," it is

good to remind ourselves, are categories that did not exist in the ancient world; indeed, Jews were sometimes called "atheists" for not worshipping the gods. The paradox that those who worshipped one god and those who worshipped many in the ancient world might nonetheless have more in common with each other than with us can be an unsettling thought. It is this problem that has made even defining what is meant by "monotheism" difficult. And so it is possible that devotion to one God was accepted by virtually all Jews, but the implications of what was involved may have been defined and interpreted differently by different individuals and/or groups within Judaism. In other words, it may be that Jews were united in a distinctive devotion to one God, and yet that devotion may not have been felt to be incompatible with the various practices that modern scholars have often considered to be evidence of heterodox or syncretistic Judaism.

I shall develop a provisional working definition of what might be meant by "Hellenistic Jewish monotheism," but at this stage it is important to emphasize that the evidence may be compatible with more than one of the views summarized above. Finding Jewish texts from this period which take for granted that only one God ought to be worshipped, as well as Jewish inscriptions indicating the recognition of the existence of other divine figures, is not necessarily incompatible with any of the aforementioned interpretations.[4] It is my aim in this chapter to focus on the role of *worship* as a defining factor and to determine which of the possible views has "the best fit" when considered in light of the available data, both textual and epigraphic. The willingness of some Jews to face martyrdom rather than offer sacrifice to foreign deities clearly indicates that this is an important place to look in seeking the make-or-break issues in defining the exclusive devotion of at least some Jews to their God alone. It is the extent and character of this dividing line that we seek to delineate and clarify.

Two major questions need to be answered in order to make a decision on this matter:

1. Had devotion to one God alone become a generally accepted Jewish viewpoint, or was it still the viewpoint of a minority or a relatively slight majority?
2. If the Jews were on the whole united in their devotion to a single God, then what made this different from the practices of other peoples in that time?[5]

In other words, we are left with the question of *whether* Judaism was in any sense monotheistic in this period, and if so, *how* (in the absence of the modern terminology of monotheism) this devotion to a single God alone was delineated from other viewpoints.

The best place to begin seems to be with the perception of outsiders, that is, of non-Jews. If the texts we have which call for the worship of only one God represent the work of a minority that was limited either numerically or geographically, then it may be expected that the features they were promoting may not have been identified as typically or quintessentially Jewish by outsiders. On the other hand, if most Jews held to a set of beliefs that set them apart from others in their primarily polytheistic world, then the existence of a small group that most would regard as "apostates" would be unlikely to affect the general perception of the characteristics of Judaism. By giving importance—although by no means sole importance—to the perception of Judaism attested by non-Jewish authors in this period, we may be able to identify elements of "common Judaism," if there was indeed such a thing in this period, without thereby undermining the existence and importance of diversity within Judaism.[6]

Thus let us begin to consider the references to the Jewish understanding of God or the gods in non-Jewish authors of the Hellenistic age. The first relevant author is Hecataeus of Abdera, who, writing about 300 BCE, makes the following points:

1. The Jews acknowledge only "heaven" as divine.
2. Jews reject the making of images of God or the gods.
3. They are in these respects, and in others of their customs, different from other peoples.[7]

Hecataeus' testimony is significant, yet we must be wary of making too much of his account unless we find it substantiated by additional evidence. I say this for several reasons. First, in the case of Hecataeus' account of the Jewish people, we are dealing with a sort of "first contact" scenario (not in an absolute sense but in the sense of a first examination of the Jewish people by a Greek ethnographer). For this reason, misunderstandings are likely. It has also been suggested that Hecataeus may have gone into his investigation with a set of questions that in all likelihood imposed a particular slant on the interpretation of any answers given.[8] But in addition to that, we do not know if Hecataeus spent time examining Jewish customs himself or simply spoke to some figure of authority in one Jewish community whose answers may have been based on a scriptural ideal rather than on real-life practice in his time. Of course, if there had been practice blatantly contradicting this account readily and publicly observable, then Hecataeus might have noted this. But perhaps he has. In stating that since Babylonian and Persian times Jewish customs have been changed, one possibility is that he is attempting to account for a contrast between the values of Mosaic monotheism and aniconism presented to him verbally and a different sort of worship that he observed among the Jewish populace at some point. Hecataeus' evidence can thus be interpreted in more than one way, and so without other clearer evidence, it would be unwise to place too much weight on his testimony alone. Be that as it may, if we can in fact confirm Hecataeus' information, then what he wrote suggests that it was possible to regard the rejection of images and the recognition of only one God as distinctive features of the Jewish people and religion at least as early as about 300 BCE.

Moving along chronologically, let us next consider the testimony of Manetho, an Egyptian author writing in the third century BCE.[9] Manetho's references are clearly polemical and are reported by Josephus in an opposing polemical context. Thus we find ourselves dealing with a source that is far more problematic than Hecataeus, and were it not for Manetho's importance because of his early date, we would be tempted to set his testimony aside and move on to other sources. It is nonetheless noteworthy that he appears to confirm what Hecateus says about the Jewish people and their religion. Manetho accuses that the ancestors of the Jewish people who lived in Egypt not only did not worship the Egyptian gods but also defaced their images, and although there is no reason to think this claim was historically true, nevertheless it assumes Jewish hatred for images of the gods, and this is thus an important piece of evidence regarding Egyptian perception of Jewish religion in Egypt in the third century BCE.

I began with Hecataeus and Manetho because they are the earliest two sources from the Hellenistic era, sources which (as we have seen) are not entirely unproblematic. Luckily, later authors consistently confirm what we see in the two earliest sources. Lester Grabbe summarizes the evidence: "The Greek and Roman writers are universal in proclaiming Jewish worship of one God. Although this God is sometimes identified with Jove . . . or even Dionysus . . . , the sources always emphasize how different Jews are from other people, and they are especially astonished at the lack of imagery in Jewish worship."[10] Although there are occasional mentions of "gods" or "temples" in the plural in Greek descriptions of Judaism, a good argument can be made that this represents an instinctive language used by the non-Jewish authors in question, rather than an accurate depiction of the Jewish religion. Indeed, such plurals are found even in authors (like Hecataeus) who nonetheless acknowledge Jewish adherence to only one God.

Those non-Jewish authors who do not appear to be deliberately polemicizing against or satirizing the Jewish faith and people describe their religion as being focused on only one God and as rejecting images. What this means, and how it relates to the textual and epigraphic evidence from Jewish sources from this period, must now be considered. Although both non-Jewish and Jewish sources speak of the God in question as "the God of the Jews" and in other such ways, there are both Jewish and non-Jewish sources which emphasize that the God in question is "God Most High," the same God recognized by non-Jews under other names such as Zeus or Dis.[11] In thinking about the distinctiveness of Judaism, and whether the anachronistic terminology of "monotheism" is appropriately applied to it, it is important to question the assumption that Jewish monotheism was inherently exclusive. Non-Jewish authors emphasize the distinctiveness of Judaism, but this tends to have to do with its *aniconism* rather than with the deity worshipped per se. Even Jewish texts are not averse to identifying their own God, God Most High, as the God whom philosophers and even pagans acknowledge in the same role under different names. See, for example, the Letter of Aristeas, in which the author asserts that the Jews worship the same God that others also acknowledge as head of the pantheon—the name may be different, but the figure denoted is not.[12] Most if not all of the Jewish polemic against Gentiles and their worship which stems from this period does not focus on the issue of polytheism abstractly defined, or on the names or concepts used for God, but on the issue of idolatry.[13]

If iconic worship was the big stumbling block, rather than the particular name by which God was called, then we can account reasonably well for both the flexibility and the intransigence expressed in Jewish sources from this period. On the one hand, the idea of a single God Most High was a potential point of agreement with others in the Hellenistic world. On the other hand, aniconic worship was probably a much more deeply rooted Israelite tradition than the Deuteronomic proscription of worship of other gods.[14] Worshipping the one true God under a different name, without idols, would probably not have been felt to be antithetical to either of the first two commandments. But at any rate, it is important to always keep in mind that these two commandments delineate two issues that were considered separate by many if not all within early Judaism: the prohibition of representations of God and the offering of sacrificial worship exclusively to the one true God and to him alone. The latter presumably could have been engaged in in many forms, using many names, as long as no images were directly involved. These considerations and distinctions are crucial if we are to formulate a view of Jewish devotion to one God in this period without retrojecting anachronistic categories. Nevertheless, I will continue to use the term "monotheism" as a convenient shorthand for "Jewish devotion to one God alone." But now we must attempt to define the form that devotion took and explore its breadth or narrowness, its exclusiveness and inclusiveness.

Although various authors emphasize or play down the distinctions between Jews and others on matters of religion in the Hellenistic age, some distinctiveness is generally either assumed or explicitly asserted by both sides in the literature of this period. This is all the more striking in view of the existence of what has been called ";the common theology of the ancient Near East." It seems that most peoples believed there was a single god who was above all others, just as was the case within Judaism. And as for the rhetoric of monotheism, in contexts of worship one often addressed the deity in an extravagant manner, saying that there is no other god, or at least no other like him or her.[15] With the situation being thus, one wonders precisely what the distinctive features of Jewish devotion to one God were that made it appear distinctive to outsiders, and how they may be identified, defined, and appropriately delineated. Larry Hurtado helpfully suggests that worship can be regarded as the defining factor: Those who not only believe there is one supreme god above all others, but worship only that god, are "monotheists."[16] This is in principle a helpful definition, and it seems to have great potential to do justice to the data from both Jewish and non-Jewish sources of the period. Further clarification is essential, however. As Hurtado points out, the Greek word for "worship" (*proskynēsis*) covers a broad range of activities, from bowing before another person to full-blown cultic sacrificial worship. The former was not universally regarded by Jews as prohibited to all figures other than God, while the latter may well have been. So the question becomes where Hellenistic Jews drew the line— and of course whether they all drew the line in the same place. Hurtado draws it somewhere roughly midway between the extremes of meaning of "worship"; he speaks specifically of *cultic* worship, by which he means not only sacrificial worship but also prayer, hymnic adoration, invocation, and other practices. I suspect that, if there was a line to be drawn (and there may have been a diversity of opinions on this subject in this period), the line would have been drawn at or near *sacrificial worship.* This, it seems to me, was in this period in the history of the Jewish people, one of the two generally accepted make-or-break issues, the other being iconic worship.

The Jewish practice of wearing amulets invoking the names of angels, and in some cases also foreign deities, is a useful test case of this point.[17] It is clear that many Jews in this period considered it appropriate to address and invoke angelic figures in direct speech addressed to them. Yet this has often been assumed to be a syncretistic practice, a departure from strict Jewish monotheism. One significant piece of evidence that this assumption is wrong is a Jewish funeral stele from Delos dating from the late second or early first century BCE, which begins by invoking God Most High but continues by addressing the Lord and the angels of God in the vocative.[18] That this was not an isolated instance is clearly indicated by the fact that the exact same text, with a different name of the deceased, has been found on another stele.[19] And so, rather than being an unusual instance, this was perhaps a standard funerary inscription for this particular Jewish Diaspora community of the Hellenistic age.[20] Thus if worship in the broad sense of invocation or prayer had served to define Jewish devotion to one God, then we would have to acknowledge the widespread persistence of Jewish polytheism well into the Hellenistic age. However, it seems to me preferable to suggest that in this period and even in later times, many forms of acknowledgment of, and interaction with, figures understood to be subordinate to God Most High were considered compatible with Jewish monotheism. Both the common theology of the ancient world, with a single high god above all others, and the Jewish view, which tended to think of God enthroned above a hierarchy of angels, were patterned on the way society was organized. God, at the top, paralleled the king or emperor to whom one owed one's ultimate political allegiance. On a day-to-day basis, however, one did not normally have to deal with the king directly but with lower functionaries and officials. Likewise, while one owed one's allegiance ultimately to God Most High, this did not by definition exclude the necessity of interacting with the local deities or angelic figures whose authority more directly presided over a particular region or aspect of life. Certainly even today this continues to be the way things are perceived in the popular piety of a number of monotheistic traditions. At any rate, provided that one's acknowledgment of God Most High as sole supreme ruler was delineated by the sacrificial worship of this God and of him alone, one could appeal to lower functionaries for intervention in certain cases as appropriate without in any way feeling that one was compromising monotheism.[21]

Moving on from this point, if one could interact with angels denoted as such in the Jewish tradition, what would have seemed different about addressing or interacting with other figures from the Greco-Roman pantheon, similarly conceived? One example from the archaeological record is a talisman with medusa found in a Jewish grave from Roman times.[22] Similarly, in 2 Maccabees 12:39–40 we are told that when "Judas and his men went to take up the bodies of the fallen and to bring them back to lie with their kinsmen in the sepulchers of their fathers, then under the tunic of every one of the dead they found sacred tokens of the idols of Jamnia, which the law forbids the Jews to wear." Of course, this in all likelihood represents a literary topos, based on stories from the Hebrew Bible like the account of the siege of Ai (Joshua 7). It was a more attractive way of explaining the losses in the battle than simply acknowledging that it came down to numbers and strategy. Nevertheless, even if there is no historical core to the story, the scenario envisaged was clearly not considered entirely implausible by the author. The story is presumably composed to warn against a practice either known to exist or likely to be considered appealing by at least some Jews. We thus have a confirmation that some felt it appropriate to wear amulets, talismans, and other such items which invoked non-Jewish deities. The author of 2 Maccabees, on the other hand, considers the practice unacceptable. So in focusing on sacrificial worship as *the* defining feature of Jewish exclusive devotion to only one God, I am not suggesting that no one felt that there were other issues of importance, other dividing lines. All I am asserting is that on the question of sacrificial worship there appears to have been general agreement, while on other matters, like amulets invoking other gods, there may not have been universal agreement—or any universally recognized religious authority that could decide the matter and define the practice as either orthodox or heterodox for the Jews of this period. But Jews who sacrificed only to God Most High and yet wore amulets invoking angels or gods, and Jews who sacrificed only to God Most High and did not wear amulets, would have seemed equally distinctive to Gentile observers who were accustomed to engage in the iconic sacrificial worship of more than one deity.

Another piece of relevant data from this period is the earliest known Jewish individual from the Hellenistic era, Moschion son of Moschion, who sets free his slave at the behest of two gods who address him in a dream.[23] Of course, Moschion does not directly appeal to or invoke other deities—he simply follows the commands they give him in a dream. Nevertheless, this inscription shows the recognition by a Jewish individual of both the existence and the authority of figures other than God

Most High in a way that is surely indicative of a characteristic of Jewish piety in this period. There was simply no way one could go through life without dealing with the "lower functionaries" responsible for the region one was living in. If, as at least one biblical passage seemed to suggest, God had appointed the "sons of God" over the various nations (Deut. 32:8, according to the LXX), then to assume one could avoid all interaction with these figures while living in the Diaspora may have seemed not only unthinkable but also unbiblical.

We have seen thus far that it would have been entirely conceivable for Jews in this period, on the one hand, to define their devotion to their own God and him alone through their offering of sacrificial worship to no others, and on the other hand, to invoke, recognize, obey, and interact with other figures, since they are presumably subordinate to (and thus no threat to the authority and unique status of) the one true God.[24] Let us now turn our attention to the Jewish inscriptions thanking "God" in a temple of Pan in Egypt from the Hellenistic age.[25] Couldn't one safely assume that this represents an example of Jewish "apostasy"? Not necessarily. Although this seems to cross even the dividing line of sacrificial worship as I have previously defined it, we shall soon see that matters are not so simple. Of course, in theory one could take *Ioudaios* in both instances as merely a geographic indicator—in which case these may be "Judeans" (i.e., Gentiles from Judea) rather than "Jews," and then for all intents and purposes the inscriptions would be irrelevant to the subject of this study. This seems rather unlikely, however. Thus in interpreting the significance of these inscriptions, one is forced to do justice to the fact that those who had these inscriptions made consciously chose to identify themselves as Jews. This is perhaps equivalent to someone today identifying himself as a Christian in a plaque indicating he donated money to the construction of a mosque. Some might feel that his action is antithetical to the teachings of his own religion, but the fact that he chose to identify himself explicitly as a Christian on the plaque suggests he is making a self-conscious statement. To be more specific, the person in question would be emphasizing through his very action that what he has done is not incompatible with his Christian identity. A similar point presumably must apply to the inscriptions from the temple of Pan. Why else even mention being Jewish?

The self-identification as *Ioudaios* may hint that some, perhaps most, who bore the same self-identification would have been uncomfortable with what was being done. But this is not the only possible explanation. Another possibility is that these two individuals singled themselves out as Jews because they were felt by local worshippers of

Pan to be outsiders both from an ethno-geographic and a religious perspective. It might be speculated that some special arrangement might have been made with the priests of Pan in this area, allowing local Jews to worship "God" in their temple. Pan had come to be thought of by many as a universal God, and it would not have been unnatural for Jews to make some sort of identification with their own God. As long as we are speculating about the background to these inscriptions, we may ask a further question that raises a tantalizing possibility, even if from our own historical standpoint the question can never be answered with certainty. Would priests of Pan have been willing to accept offerings from Jews with some stipulation attached that the sacrifice not be offered directly to an idol? It is certainly not beyond imagining that, whether for the sake of profit or the sake of showing hospitality and understanding toward Jews living in the area, the local priests might be sympathetic to such an arrangement. As already emphasized, this suggestion is entirely speculative. Nevertheless, I hope it is clear that even the inscriptions from the temple of Pan may not have been considered to involve an abandonment of Jewish monotheism. Had these individuals believed they were abandoning their ancestral faith and culture, it seems likely that they would have sought to integrate themselves into their new identity and would simply have ceased to identify themselves as "Jews." While their actions tested the limits of the acceptable, and may possibly have been frowned upon by other Jews, there is no evidence that these individuals either left the Jewish community of their own free will or were forced to do so.[26] When all is said and done, these intriguing inscriptions retain the character of exceptions that prove the rule.

One might perhaps be tempted, in light of such evidence as these inscriptions, to suggest that there were groups of Jews in the Diaspora who never came under the influence of the monotheistic revolution that took place during the late pre-exilic period and thereafter. This explanation of the evidence, however, must be rejected. It is unlikely that such Jewish individuals and communities in the Diaspora failed to be influenced by the Deuteronomic teachings that were emphasized in Jerusalem and Judea in this period. For in order for an expatriate community to maintain its identity, some sort of ongoing link to the motherland is essential. And so it is better to regard these inscriptions as simply another piece of evidence that there was great potential within Judaism for their "monotheistic" tradition to be interpreted inclusively rather than exclusively. Or if one concludes that such instances actually crossed the line and betrayed Jewish "monotheism," then these instances illustrate another important point: Participation in Greco-Roman society involved constant contact with pagan cultic activities. All but a small minority may have agreed that one should not offer sacrifice in temples other than the one in Jerusalem. However, it is clear from Jewish sources that there were differing views regarding just how far one might go in participating in the civic and cultural events of the time, since some contact with Greco-Roman polytheism and idols was inevitable.[27] And because meals involved at least the likelihood of contact with food sacrificed to idols, we find in later Judaism and Christianity debates relating not just specifically to sacrificial worship, but also to questions of meals and eating as well. Thus, in drawing the dividing line at sacrificial worship, there were still ambiguities relating to just what it might or might not be appropriate for Jews to do.

Toward the end of the Hellenistic and beginning of the Roman period, the Maccabean crisis serves as a catalyst for some significant changes in the outlook of many Jews. The story of these events is well known and is told in the books of 1 and 2 Maccabees. In response to the attempt to impose changes in religious practice on the Jewish people, a backlash occurs, one that could with some legitimacy perhaps be called "fundamentalist." In this context, a "monotheistic" slant in an even narrower sense is given to the form of Jewish piety officially sponsored and sanctioned by the Hasmonean rulers. In the ancient world, popular piety was every bit as likely to transgress the bounds of what leaders and theologians considered appropriate or "orthodox" forms of worship as it is today. However, when it comes to official forms of religion, such as sacrifice, then royal decrees and laws had a much bigger part to play. It is in the context of the Maccabean age that one finds clearer moves being made in the direction of monotheism in the stricter sense in which the word is used today: all forms of acknowledgment of foreign gods are to be avoided.[28] As already noted, the author of 2 Maccabees (who was a supporter of the Hasmonean dynasty) considered the practice of wearing amulets invoking other gods to be an unacceptable practice. However, to presume that, prior to the radical nationalistic fervor that ensued in the wake of the uprising in the time of Antiochus Epiphanes, Jewish religion had the same *sort* of monotheistic emphasis, seems seriously questionable. Even afterward, the attempt to impose a more stringent interpretation of Jewish monotheism is only partially successful, and the practices discussed in this chapter continue to persist well into the Roman and rabbinic periods of Jewish history. Further discussions, debates, and developments take place in the context of rabbinic Judaism, after the period in which the New Testament was written, and I will return to these matters in chapter 6. But to summarize, in my view it is not entirely inappropriate to describe the Jewish people in the Hellenistic age as "monotheistic" even prior to the time of the Maccabees. The key issue is to recognize that what the worship of one God alone meant during most of that era is not necessarily the same thing that it meant in other periods, nor the same thing that it is interpreted to mean today.[29]

When one considers the character of Jewish beliefs in this period, Fredriksen appears to have been right to say that, in relation to modern definitions, "all monotheists in the ancient world were polytheists." However, this has led some to the conclusion that there was no significant fundamental difference between Judaism and other religions in the Hellenistic age or even later. This suggestion simply flies in the face of the sense of distinctiveness and of exclusive devotion to one God expressed (and so frequently simply assumed and taken for granted) in Jewish texts from Ezra-Nehemiah to Ben Sira to the books of the Maccabees and beyond. I therefore suggest that in this period Judaism did have something that might be called "monotheism" (although some might prefer to call it "monolatry"), but it was far more flexible than the definitions of monotheism used in later Jewish thought and in our own time. The sacrificial worship of the one God without images was the make-or-break issue. In other areas, one often finds that attempts were made to single out other issues as also important, but there is nothing like a consensus on these matters. Some apparently considered it unacceptable to wear amulets invoking anyone other than Israel's God Most High. But not everyone agreed, and it was conceivable to a Jewish author writing from the more exclusive standpoint that those Jews who considered such amulets acceptable would nonetheless have given their lives fighting for Jewish religious freedom and for the elimination of idols or altars that contravened the Law of Moses from the Jerusalem temple. Or as we find in various pieces of apocalyptic literature, some would "worship" angels in the sense of bowing before them while others strongly warned against this practice.

With this understanding of monotheism in the Judaism of this period—as meaning all those who considered that animal sacrifices were to be offered to only one God—it is possible to make the best sense of the available evidence and find ways of doing justice to both the sense of a common religious identity expressed by Jews in this period as well as to the diversity of practices evidenced both in texts and in material culture. Thus the evidence points to there having been a belief held in common by most (if not indeed all) Jews of this period, which made it apparent to non-Jewish observers that this people's belief and custom distinguished them from the norm of mainstream Hellenistic religion. One unifying core belief (and there may have been others) was the belief that God Most High, whom the Jews worship, is the only rightful recipient of sacrifice. To offer sacrifice to an idol, or to a god felt to be competing for the honor due only to the one true God, would have been rejected by most if not all those in this period who bore the name "Jews." However, within this unifying "monotheism" or "monolatry," there was also room for significant diversity.[30]

Moving into the Roman era, we find Jews (and eventually Christians) apparently united on these core beliefs and practices. However, we shall also find significant new developments within both of these offspring of Hellenistic Judaism's heritage as we move into New Testament times and beyond. Monotheism meant different things in different ages and within different traditions. But in emphasizing this diversity, it would be wrong to neglect the underlying unity evidenced throughout available sources regarding Hellenistic Judaism, namely, the core belief that only one God is to be offered sacrificial worship, the form of worship par excellence in the ancient world.[31] Whether one calls this "monotheism" or "monolatry" in the end matters little, except in one important sense. It would be wrong to use terms other than monotheism for early Jewish devotion to one God if these other terms are understood to denigrate this form of belief, as though it were something not fully formed, merely a step on the path toward monotheism in a fuller sense, which is understood to be the ultimate goal. Such judgments are made by those who have stood under the influence of a long tradition of exclusive monotheism in the contemporary sense and who judge the past in light of that upbringing. Yet it cannot be emphasized enough that for the Jews of this period, their exclusive worship of God Most High and him alone constituted a highly advanced form of monotheism, presumably the most advanced form of monotheism in existence in their time. In practicing it, they felt themselves to simply be following the teaching of their Scriptures, and faithfully worshipping and serving their God. These were devoted monotheists who were often willing to give their lives rather than compromise their devotion to one God alone. They ought not to be regarded individuals who had compromised or abandoned their faith, simply because some of their beliefs and practices came to be defined in later times as unacceptable or unorthodox. Indeed, one could argue that to worship one's God faithfully and exclusively when he is not felt to be the only god is perhaps a greater achievement than doing so when one is convinced no other god exists at all. But such value judgments are probably altogether out of place here. My aim has been simply to describe the form of devotion to God found in Hellenistic Judaism. The Jews of this period, if not exactly modern monotheists, were more than merely "polytheists who worshipped only one God," since the Jewish literature of this period emphasizes not only that one God alone is worthy of worship but also that (as God Most High) their God is incomparably greater than any other god. Although the meaning of the word needs to be carefully qualified in relation to this period, it is my conviction that monotheism remains the best of the available terms to describe Jewish devotion to one God in the Greco-Roman era. The next step will be to see how early Christian beliefs and practice compare to the form of devotion to only one God we find evidenced in Jewish sources from this period. As we shall see in the chapters that follow, the New Testament sources appear to fit nicely within the bounds of Jewish monotheism as we have come to identify it in this chapter.

3 Monotheism and the Letters
Attributed to Paul

In examining the view(s) of God held by the early Christians, it is to the letters of Paul that we turn first, since they provide our earliest written sources. Although it might seem more natural to begin with the historical figure of Jesus himself, it is only through writings from this time period that we can gain access to him. All the early Christian texts at our disposal in the New Testament reflect not only historical realities from the time of Jesus but also beliefs held by Christians in the time these works were written. A study of the view of God held by the historical Jesus would for this reason probably require a book of its own in order to do justice to the historical evidence.[1] For the present purposes, therefore, we must limit ourselves to the evidence of early Christian texts. And so it is to the earliest Christian author, the apostle Paul, that we now turn our attention.

One of the most important passages to be considered is 1 Corinthians 8:6, where Paul makes use of the Shema, the fundamental affirmation of Jewish allegiance to one God alone. Found in Deuteronomy 6:4, it states, "Hear O Israel! The LORD our God, the LORD is one!" While there have been some interesting discussions about the meaning of the phrase in its original context and the possibility of slightly different translations, for our purposes we need not pursue such matters. By the time of the origins of Christianity, there can be no doubt that this verse had a creedal significance for Jewish communities, and we know how it was translated into Greek in the Septuagint for the benefit of Greek-speaking Jews, which is very close to the usual rendering into English in our time. It is the question of what Paul does with the Shema here that is of interest to us.

In the view of the majority of New Testament scholars, in 1 Corinthians 8:6 Paul has "split the Shema," the traditional affirmation of Israel's faith in one God, in order to include Jesus Christ within it. Thus James Dunn writes that Paul "splits the *Shema* (Deut. 6.4), the Jewish confession of monotheism, between God the Father and Christ the Lord in a way that has no earlier parallel."[2] Similarly Tom Wright has affirmed that this verse "functions as a Christian redefinition of the Jewish confession of faith, the *Shema*."[3] He further explains, "Paul has placed Jesus *within* an explicit statement, drawn from the Old Testament's quarry of emphatically monotheistic texts, of the doctrine that Israel's God is the one and only God . . . Paul has redefined it christologically, producing what we can only call a sort of christological monotheism."[4]

In this chapter, we will look at evidence that challenges the idea that Jesus has here been included *inside* rather than *alongside* the Shema. The main difficulty with the view that Paul has "split the Shema" to produce a "Christological monotheism" (whatever that might mean) is that it does not do justice to the nature of the Shema itself. The Shema reads: "Hear O Israel, Yahweh [is] our God, Yahweh is one," or in a rendering that follows the LXX more closely, "Hear O Israel, the Lord our God, the Lord is one." It would be very difficult for Paul to distinguish between "God" in the Shema as referring to the Father and "Lord" in the Shema as referring to the Son, since the Shema clearly identifies "Lord" (rendering the tetragrammaton) and "God." That Paul could do this in passing, without explaining it or defending it, seems very unlikely indeed. The fact of the matter is that Paul does not say that there is one God who is both Father and Son; he says rather that there is *one God* and *also one Lord*. The fact that a human figure is called "Lord" does not of course imply for Paul that God is thereby divested of his lordship. No, indeed; all things (other than God) are subjected to Christ because God has placed them there (1 Cor. 15:25–28). However, Paul does apply to Jesus the designation that was commonly used in the place of the name of God, namely, "Lord." Of course, this word had a range of meanings and nuances running all the way from "sir" to "Yahweh." Nevertheless, it is not inappropriate to ask whether, if Christ could be called "one Lord" without denying that God is "Lord," the reverse could also apply. In other words, is it possible that the reference to "one God" ought not to be understood exclusively, but inclusively, as including Jesus as well? Grammatical considerations, while essential, will not on their own be sufficient to answer this question. Much will also depend on what we think Paul's readers could be expected to understand and presuppose.

As far as grammatical considerations are concerned, there is a sense in which *either* part of Paul's statement could be taken on its own as a paraphrase of the Shema. The combination "one God and . . ." suggests that we are dealing with a paraphrase of the Shema with an additional affirmation added alongside it—otherwise we would surely have expected Paul to express himself differently. Theoretically, he could have written, "There is one God: the Father, from whom are all things, and the Son, through whom are all things." This would have emphasized the oneness of God while including Jesus clearly within that one God. Instead, Paul uses a statement about one God, which itself is sufficient to reiterate the point of the Shema, and then goes further to talk about "one Lord." When the oneness of God is coupled with another assertion of oneness in this way, we must look carefully to determine whether we are indeed dealing with a splitting of the Shema that is without parallel, or an addition of a second clause *alongside* the Shema, which is not in fact unparalleled in Jewish literature.

We are of course in no way denying that the Shema is in mind in 1 Corinthians 8, and that Jesus is being related to it. However, the nature of the relationship has for too long been assumed, and is in desperate need of clarification. The first part of Paul's statement in 1 Corinthians 8:6 resembles the statement of faith, probably itself a paraphrase of the Shema, found in Philo's writings: "Let us, then, engrave deep in our hearts this as the first and most sacred of commandments, to acknowledge and honor one God who is above all, and let the idea that gods are many never even reach the ears of the man whose rule of life it is to seek for truth in purity and goodness."[5] The point here is that there is one God who is incomparably "above all." Such language in early Judaism rarely if ever means that no other being may be referred to as "god," but simply that all others are (to use Paul's own phrase) merely "so-called gods" who are not worthy of comparison with the one true God. Similarly, Paul's statement slightly earlier that "there is no God but one" (1 Corinthians 8:4) closely resembles the statement in the Sibylline Oracles (3.629) that "He alone is God and there is no other." Mention may also be made of Josephus, *Jewish Antiquities* 5.112, which refers either to one God who is common to all Hebrews, or perhaps to the affirmation "God is one" as being common to all Hebrews. At any rate, it seems clear that the language of "one God" was already a well-known way of summarizing this aspect of Jewish belief. Paul uses this language of "one God" and adds to it a reference to "one Lord." It is thus the *addition* of another element alongside this traditional affirmation of Jewish monotheistic faith that we must attempt to understand.

The contrast Paul makes—between many gods and one God and many lords and one Lord—sounds like it is referring to figures in the heavenly and earthly realms, respectively, to divine beings and their earthly representatives or mediators. Paul had just referred to "so-called gods, whether in heaven or on earth" (1 Cor. 8:5), and his reference to "many gods" and "many lords" appears to be an expansion or clarification of what Paul had in mind in referring to both heavenly and earthly "so-called gods."[6] The flow of the sentence and the parallels within it become clearer when outlined as follows:

One God vs. many gods
(whether in heaven	or on earth)
many gods	many lords
One God	One Lord

Thus the "many gods" are best understood as a reference to the gods which are thought to exist in the heaven, and the "many lords" are then the rulers or lords on the earth, who represented the authority of the gods in the sphere of human existence.[7]

Paul's statement in 1 Corinthians 8:6 is best interpreted over against this aspect of contemporary Greco-Roman belief. For Christians, says Paul, there is only one God in heaven, and there is only one Lord, one agent and mediator, who rules on his behalf over all creation. That Paul is speaking about one God, the ultimate authority and source of all things, and one mediator of that authority and creative activity, is made clear by the prepositions used: "One God, *from* whom . . . and one Lord, *through* whom . . ." Paul has already affirmed that there is "no God but one," and verse 6 expands and comments on this affirmation of monotheistic faith by adding that there is also one figure appointed by God as ruler over all things.[8]

Dunn, as discussed, has asserted that what Paul does with the Shema here "has no earlier parallel." In fact, there are a number of examples of Jewish and Christian authors who draw the conclusion that, just as there is only one God, so also there must be only one mediator of a particular sort or other. Let us begin by looking first at a slightly later Christian parallel, 1 Timothy 2:5. Whether or not this letter was written by Paul himself need not concern us, since the view of God and Christ expressed seems to be seeking to remain true to Paul's legacy, on this point at least.[9] What is important for our purposes is that it shows another example of an early Christian statement of faith which asserts that there is one God and one mediator. Here—as also, I would argue, in 1 Corinthians 8:6—we have before us an expanded Shema rather than a split Shema. In other words, something has been added on the outside, alongside the Shema, rather than on the inside, into the definition of the nature of God himself. The affirmation of the oneness of God is a traditional Jewish axiom, and in 1 Timothy 2:5 we find added alongside it the additional claim that this one God has only one mediator between himself and human kind: the human being Christ Jesus. It seems appropriate to interpret the passage in 1 Corinthians along similar lines: The affirmation of "one God" represents the monotheistic confession of the Shema, and the affirmation of "one Lord" is added to it.[10]

Another example of the supplemented Shema in the Pauline corpus is found in 1 Thessalonians 1:9–10. There we find a description of conversion to Christianity that initially might serve equally well as a description of conversion to Judaism: The Thessalonians had turned from idols to serve the living and true God.[11] So far, so good. The passage then goes on to add an additional element that is distinctively Christian: They also await the return of Jesus from heaven. This second element is not added as an expansion or redefinition of the monotheistic character of Christian belief—indeed, had Paul wanted to say some such thing, we would certainly expect him to have expressed himself differently. What he says is clear: The Thessalonians had abandoned idol worship in order to serve the God whom Jews and Christians believe is the only true God, and as Christians, they further understand Jesus to be God's unique son and agent of salvation. Nothing whatsoever in this passage hints that a departure from monotheism could be envisaged by either the author or his readers. The same, I suggest, is true in 1 Corinthians 8 as well.

To clarify further that by appending something additional to the Shema one need not "split" it nor be understood to be incorporating the additional person or thing mentioned into the divine identity, we may note an example of similar language from the Hebrew Bible: 2 Samuel 7:22–24. There we find a contrast made between Yahweh and other gods in a manner not wholly unlike 1 Corinthians 8:6. In it, the affirmation that God is one ("There is no God but you") is coupled with the affirmation that there is likewise "one nation that God went out to redeem as a people for himself." I doubt whether anyone has ever suggested that in this passage the people of Israel are being included within the Shema.[12] Hopefully this example makes clear just how unnecessary it is to presume Paul to have been adding Jesus within the Shema, and also how quickly many of us today read back later theological ideas into Paul's statements, ideas that were only developed much later. In the context of his own historical setting, there is no reason that the affirmation of "One God (the creator) and one Lord (the mediator)" would necessarily have compromised Jewish monotheism or "split the Shema," any more than would the affirmation that one God implies one people of God, or that one God implies only one temple (on which see especially Josephus, *Against Apion* 2:193). This is not to deny that Paul was making an unusually exalted claim regarding Jesus—he surely was. But an exalted claim for a human being was not by definition incompatible with "monotheism."

It may perhaps be useful to provide just a couple of short examples of parallels from Jewish literature of this period, which indicate something of the range of exalted affirmations that could be made about mediator figures within the context of Jewish monotheism. We may begin with Testament of Abraham, a Jewish work (although with indications of some later Christian editing) that probably dates from the first century CE. It exists in two different versions, but both agree in attributing the role of judge of the dead to Abel the son of Adam. In chapters 12–13 in the longer version (known as Recension A), Abraham sees a judge seated on a throne who shines like the sun and judges the souls of those who have died. In the shorter version (Recension B, chaps. 10–11), the description is somewhat less grandiose, but Abel still serves as judge in a similar fashion. In both cases, a human being serves as the role of judge of human beings, a prerogative usually reserved for God. A similar role is given to the Elect One in 1 Enoch 61:8, which is in a section of this Jewish apocalyptic work that is known as the Similitudes of Enoch and is likewise believed to date from roughly the first century CE. In fact, this "son of man" is said to "judge all the works of the holy ones in heaven above," an exalted status indeed for one to attribute to a human being. In 62:9, the rulers of the earth are said to fall down before the Elect One and worship him. These statements occur within a book that nonetheless uses the language normally associated with Jewish exclusive allegiance to one God alone (see, e.g., 1 Enoch 9:4–5; 84:2–3).[13] Hurtado is of course correct to point out that in none of these instances do we find the same pattern of worship as the regular practice of a community, as was the case with early Christian reverence of Jesus. This does not necessarily indicate, however, that in the case of early Christianity we are dealing with an entirely different phenomenon. It is surely to be expected that the reaction to an experience of divine salvation in the present will be more enthusiastic than one's response to stories of salvation told about the distant past or the indeterminate future.

There is thus no real reason to regard Paul's affirmation in this passage as "Christological monotheism" rather than simply a form of "monotheistic Christology." Paul's statement about Jesus as the only Lord adds the distinctive Christian affirmation of faith "Jesus is Lord" to the traditional Jewish credo "God is one."[14] In Matthew 28:19 we see a similar process in reverse. The original baptismal practice of early Jewish Christianity appears to have been to baptize in the name of Jesus (as is attested by the book of Acts; cf. 8:16; 19:5). However, for the Gentile mission it became necessary to affirm explicitly not only faith in Jesus but also in the one God, and from such needs Matthew's "triune" formula was presumably born, the same threefold statement we meet in the Apostles' Creed and elsewhere.[15] Even though 1 Corinthians 8:6 is located in the context of a contrast with pagan polytheism, this "statement of faith" may in fact be a traditional confession which had already been formulated in a different, earlier context.[16] Just as worship of one God distinguished Jews from pagans, early Jewish Christians may have added the affirmation of one mediator in order to distinguish themselves from nonmessianic Jews. We see already in Galatians 3:19–20 the emphasis that one God implies one mediator and one united people, which in turn is understood to have the corollary that the Torah given through Moses as mediator cannot be the ultimate expression of God's purpose, since it separates Jews from Gentiles.[17]

The issue of Torah, which was so important for Paul, sheds light on another aspect of 1 Corinthians 8:6. Many see in the statement that all things are "through" the one Lord Jesus Christ an identification of Jesus with the figure of Wisdom. In this context it is appropriate to refer to the hymnic passage in Colossians 1:15–20, where Wisdom language and mediation of creation is again applied to Jesus.[18] However, this last point is significant: These things are not said of Wisdom, nor even of the preexistent Christ, but of the human being Jesus. In both cases it is the "Lord Jesus Christ" of whom such affirmations are made. The fact that such statements appear only in poetic, hymnic, and confessional contexts in the Pauline corpus is not to be ignored. Indeed, in view of the parallels between Colossians and Ephesians, it is appropriate to examine the latter to see what part corresponds to Colossians 1:15–20. There is no corresponding hymn or poem, but this fact makes the comparison all the more useful. What Colossians expresses in the language of preexistent Wisdom, Ephesians expresses in terms of God's eternal plan and of the magnificent power of God at work in Christ. If Ephesians is indicative of how the same ideas could be expressed in a more prosaic way, then we what we have here is a metaphorical expression of the conviction that God's wisdom is to be found in Christ, and that in his role as savior he takes over the functions of personified Wisdom, so that the goal of God's creation is accomplished by all things coming to be "in Christ."

The same sort of metaphorical, personified Wisdom language as is used to depict Christ in these examples from the letters of Paul, was applied by Jewish authors to Torah (cf. Baruch 4:1; Sirach 24:23). In both of these texts, prior to being identified with the Jewish Law, Wisdom is depicted in a very colorful and highly personalized manner. For example, Sirach 24:1–11 (RSV) reads:

> Wisdom will praise herself, and will glory in the midst of her people. In the assembly of the Most High she will open her mouth, and in the presence of his host she will glory: "I came forth from the mouth of the Most High, and covered the earth like a mist. I dwelt in high places, and my throne was in a pillar of cloud. Alone I have made the circuit of the vault of heaven and have walked in the depths of the abyss. In the waves of the sea, in the whole earth, and in every people and nation I have gotten a possession. Among all these I sought a resting place; I sought in whose territory I might lodge. Then the Creator of all things gave me a commandment, and the one who created me assigned a place for my tent. And he said, "Make your dwelling in Jacob, and in Israel receive your inheritance." From eternity, in the beginning, he created me, and for eternity I shall not cease to exist. In the holy tabernacle I ministered before him, and so I was established in Zion. In the beloved city likewise he gave me a resting place, and in Jerusalem was my dominion.

This description continues for several more verses, and yet the author then goes on to say in verse 24, "All this is the book of the covenant of the Most High God, the law which Moses commanded us as an inheritance for the congregations of Jacob."

It seems quite obvious to most readers of these Jewish texts that the "incarnation of Wisdom" in the Jewish Law does not refer to an actual preexistent person becoming a book. The application of Wisdom language to Jesus, therefore, need not necessarily imply more than that Paul believed God's Wisdom is to be found in Christ rather than (or in a fuller sense than) in Torah. There is no reason to think that the author of this early Christian hymn, in building on earlier Jewish use of such language, was importing into it a radically different meaning. Indeed, both the Colossians hymn and the passage from Sirach become nearly unintelligible if interpreted literally. It is hard to imagine that the "Book of the Law" literally carried out priestly service before God in the Jerusalem temple. Nor can Colossians mean that the universe came into existence after the birth of Jesus, so that it was through this human being that all things were made. Yet Colossians simply says of *Jesus*, "All things in heaven and earth were created in him."[19]

It is thus necessary either to interpret the text in a metaphorical manner, or to add additional beliefs and doctrines in the context of which the statement makes sense. There is no reason to regard it as impossible that, as the church has historically believed, what the author meant was that these things are true of *the preexistent one* who became the human being Jesus at the incarnation. Nevertheless, it is also possible, in view of the Jewish parallels, that the language used in Colossians is simply a poetical way of saying that God's Wisdom is found in Jesus. It may also express the conviction that, if all things were intended by God to find their fulfillment in Christ, then they must have been created "in him" in the very beginning in some undefined sense, since it was axiomatic that the eschatological climax of history would be a restoration of its perfect, original state. It is also to be noted that the language, while strikingly analogous to language used of God's original creation, need not necessarily mean more than that Jesus is the one through whom God's *new* creation takes place.[20] After all, there is nothing in the letters attributed to Paul comparable to the much more developed statements found in John, concerning "the one who came down from heaven, the Son of Man" (John 3:13). That the language is metaphorical seems counterintuitive to Christian readers, accustomed as we are to reading these texts in light of the doctrine of the Trinity. However, when we read Colossians 1:15–20 against the background of texts from that time period, it becomes clear that this alternative way of viewing the text merits serious consideration.

Thus we are left with two main options in interpreting this passage: that it views Jesus as the *incarnation* of Wisdom understood as a preexistent person or that it views him as the *embodiment* of God's Wisdom in a comparable but presumably greater way than the Law of Moses. In choosing between the two, the interpreter needs to determine not just what the Pauline letters say, but also what the readers of these letters would have assumed Wisdom language to have referred to. It is true that, in the letters of Paul, there is little if any use of preexistence language outside of poetic and other metaphorical contexts. However, even if these letters do not explicitly use such language, it may nonetheless be the case that early Jewish-Christian readers familiar with

Jewish ideas about Wisdom would have understood them to refer to an actual figure. A solution to this interpretative problem thus needs to be sought beyond the Pauline corpus of writings, in the writings of early Judaism.

This need not present a problem in this context, however, since the primary aim is to determine the relationship between early Christian and Jewish monotheism. Thus even if, when Paul identified Jesus with Wisdom, he understood Wisdom to be a literal, preexistent divine person or *hypostasis*, there is still no evidence that this would have involved a move beyond the bounds of first-century Jewish monotheism. Wisdom was a Jewish idea, and the language that he applies to Jesus, whether understood literally or metaphorically, was derived from that Jewish background. It is noteworthy that, whereas Paul engages in a great deal of legitimation for his view of Torah, there is no indication that he felt the need to defend himself against charges of "two powers heresy" or the abandonment of monotheism.[21] Paul clearly felt the need to defend his new faith over against the views he had previously held. Had his view of God or the exalted language he applied to Jesus been controversial from a Jewish perspective, involving an obvious departure from Jewish monotheism, then we would have expected him to engage in as rigorous a defense of this part of his Christian beliefs as he does in relation to the Law. That he does not, while admittedly an argument from silence, is not without force. It is like the dog that did not bark in the Sherlock Holmes story.

In the available Jewish texts that date from the first century of the Christian era, there is no evidence that belief in a supreme mediator or agent of God was controversial within Judaism. This is not to be explained by the lack of any universally recognized authority that could speak for Jewish "orthodoxy" in this period. Even within the context of first-century Jewish diversity, parties in conflict with one another took seriously the objections of their opponents and sought to respond to them.[22] In the case of Paul's claims about the exalted Christ, as in the case of Philo's view of the Logos as a *second god*, there is no sign that their contemporaries found their ideas to be significantly controversial, much less "heretical."[23]

What are we to make of this particular mediator figure? Are we dealing with metaphor or with a preexistent person? Whether in the writings of Philo, Jewish sapiential texts, or the letters of Paul, there is no unambiguous indication that the language of personified Wisdom is anything other than a way of referring to the one God. The personification is far more elaborate and developed in relation to Wisdom and

Word than in texts that speak of the "arm of the Lord" or other such attributes of God. However, it probably still belongs in the same category. Nevertheless, in seeking to decide between "metaphor" and "reality," we are once again in danger of imposing distinctions on the literature of this time that its authors and readers would not have made. As shall be discussed in the next chapter in further detail, authors in this period write about Wisdom, Word, and Spirit as though they are separate individuals from God while also referring to them in ways that indicate they are continuous with the one God and not truly separate entities. They can be spoken of by the very same authors as being separate and subordinate, and yet as none other than attributes and aspects of God himself. From our standpoint in history, looking back on a different world from many centuries later, it may prove impossible to answer these questions. What we can say with certainty, however, is that these ancient Jewish and Christian ways of speaking will not fit neatly into our contemporary categories of either "metaphor" or "person."

This should come as no surprise to those familiar with theological study. Theology has always left recourse to the idea of "mystery." Many ancient Jewish and Christian authors would have agreed that God transcends the ability of human reason to comprehend. One of the criticisms often made of the doctrine of the Trinity as formulated by the Council of Nicaea, or the doctrine of the person of Christ as formulated at Chalcedon, is that these doctrines attempt to say two things at once that cannot be logically held together. Phrases like "three persons, one substance" and "one person, two natures" stretch human language to breaking point. Should it be any surprise that some of the early precursors to these ideas are equally fraught with the same tensions? Nevertheless, there seem to have been at least some Jewish authors who used the language of Wisdom in a purely metaphorical way, as only a personification and nothing more. Texts that fall into this category—such as Sirach and Baruch—are arguably closer to the thought world of the apostle Paul than are the writings of Philo. And so, given that Paul's letters seem to reserve Wisdom language for metaphorical expressions of devotion, there is no real reason to assume that this language was intended to be taken literally. Yet as we have seen, this question is completely independent of the question of Paul's monotheism, since those authors who did use (or at least, who *may have* used) this language in a more literal fashion also fit firmly within the bounds of Jewish monotheism as it was understood, believed, and practiced in the first century.

We have seen much evidence indicating that the language applied to Jesus in the Pauline letters would not have involved a departure from the Jewish monotheism of the time. Yet there remains another piece of evidence that some will consider to tell decisively against my argument in this chapter, namely, the fact that Paul uses "Lord" (Greek *kyrios*) to represent the divine name (i.e., the tetragrammaton) that has been given to Jesus. This is seen most clearly in Philippians 2:10–11, where Paul applies to Jesus language that is applied to God in the Jewish Scriptures.[24] This use of "Lord" as the divine name can easily be misunderstood, however. In at least some streams of thought within the diversity of first-century Judaism, it was not felt to be incompatible with monotheism for God's supreme agent to bear God's name as part of his empowerment to serve in this capacity.[25] A striking example, which provides an instructive parallel to Paul's own statements, is the case of the angel Yahoel in Apocalypse of Abraham. The name Yahoel is clearly made up of the two divine names, Yah(weh) and El. Yet the reason the angel bears this name is not because he has been confused with or absorbed into God but because the angel has been *given* the divine name by God. This is made clear in Apocalypse of Abraham 10:3, 8, where God is portrayed as saying, "Go, Yahoel of the same name, through the mediation of my ineffable name." This presumably represents an interpretation of Exodus 23:21, which refers to an angel in whom God's name dwells. Nevertheless, David Capes has actually suggested that when the name "Yahoel" appears in the hymn in Apocalypse of Abraham 17:8–14, the angel is in fact being included in the worship of God.[26] But "Yahoel" in this context is the name of God, the name which the angel bears.[27] That this is the case is clear from 17:2, 7, which depicts the angel as kneeling with Abraham and reciting the hymn of worship with him. The angel is among the worshippers of God and is not confused with God, even though as God's agent he bears the name of God himself.[28] Paul's statement about Jesus in Philippians 2 is comparable; upon his exaltation, God has *given* to Jesus the *name that is above every name,* that is, the name of God.

That Paul's application of the divine name "Lord" and of Yahweh texts from the Hebrew Bible to Jesus is intended to present Jesus as God's agent, who shares in God's rule and authority, becomes clear when one considers Romans 14:9–11, where Paul takes up the language of Isaiah 45:23 once again, but here emphasizes that the throne of judgment is ultimately God's, even though Christ is the Lord through whom judgment is carried out. In 1 Corinthians 15:27–28, Paul makes clear the roles played by Jesus and God: Jesus is the "(son of) man" to whom all things are to be subjected. That is to say, Jesus is the representative of humankind whom God has chosen to be his agent and mediator of judgment, and through whom he intends to bring all things into subjection to himself.[29] Thus however united and "at one" with God the agent may be, the two remain ultimately distinguishable for Paul. Monotheism is preserved not because Jesus is absorbed into God or included in the divine identity but because even though Jesus reigns over absolutely everything else on God's behalf, God himself is not subjected to Christ, but Christ is subjected to God.[30]

Let us consider the bowing and confessing which Philippians 2:10–11 says will be offered to Jesus. As noted, several recent studies emphasize the importance of *worship* as the factor which, in Israel's mind, distinguished its God from all others.[31] And as noted in that context, this appears to be an accurate assessment, if one thinks exclusively of the *sacrificial worship* which took place in the Jerusalem temple. There is no evidence of any organized sacrificial worship of a figure other than Yahweh in the Jerusalem cultus in early Judaism. However, the act of *proskunēsis*, of prostrating oneself before another human figure who was a representative of Yahweh, was apparently never objected to in early Judaism. The two qualifications I have included are important. The Book of Revelation objects to prostration before angels, since it could be taken to imply that humans are inferior to angels (Rev. 19:10; 22:8–9); however, the same action before human beings is not problematic (Rev. 3:9).[32] And whereas Philo (*Embassy to Gaius* 116) and the LXX of Esther 13:12–14 object to the practice of prostrating oneself before pagan rulers who in pride had set themselves up against God, prostration before God's king or agent is apparently perfectly acceptable in 1 Chronicles 29:20, 1 Enoch 62:9, and Ezekiel the Tragedian's *Exagogē* 79–80.[33] In all of these latter instances the figure either sits on the throne of God or is enthroned alongside God in a position second only to God himself. The depiction in Philippians 2 of Jesus enthroned in heaven, given God's name and ruling as God's vice regent, parallels ideas found in other early Jewish writings. While some would regard all of these authors as having compromised monotheism, once again it must be noted that monotheism is itself a modern term, and one which should not be imposed anachronistically on the historical data from this period. Early Judaism appears to have felt that belief in a large host of angels, exalted patriarchs, and personified divine attributes was not incompatible with belief in one God who was above all other figures and alone worthy of sacrificial worship.[34] Paul's understanding of Jesus appears to fit within this context.

To put it another way, readings of Philippians 2:6–11 which emphasize the exalted status of Jesus and the application to him of language which applied to Yahweh in Isaiah tend to emphasize only part of what this passage actually says. That Paul believed Jesus occupied this exalted status can hardly be questioned. However, this text makes equally clear that Jesus was exalted by God to this position, and the clear implication is that this was a position he did not previously occupy. God exalted him, and when he did so, he gave Jesus his own divine name, which again he did not previously bear. The reason for conferring this exalted status on Jesus is that every knee should bow and every tongue confess that Jesus is Lord. The only way to interpret this text in a manner that does justice to what it actually says is to understand that God here shares his own exalted status with Jesus in a way that does not jeopardize God's ultimate supremacy. The reason it is so difficult for us as contemporary readers to accept this apparently plain meaning of the text (apart from the presupposition most of us have of doctrines developed and defined in the later church) is presumably that in our contemporary understanding of monotheism, God either cannot or would not share such prerogatives. However, this assumption does not appear to have been shared by either Paul or his Jewish contemporaries who depict other figures as bearing the divine name or sitting on God's throne. In ancient Judaism, God could empower his agent to wield his full power and authority, *precisely because* any figure so empowered always remained by definition subject and subordinate to the one empowering him, namely, God.

The reasons why God might so empower his agent are not difficult to imagine. First, it leaves nothing outside of the scope of the agent's authority. In the case of early Christianity, the community of believers associated with Jesus would have thus had absolute confidence in him as God's unique representative. In thinking of the king as God's agent in ancient Israel, the emphasis on the potential of the Davidic king to bring all nations into subjection highlighted the special status of Israel. The authority and sovereignty given by God to his agent also served to enhance the honor and prestige of the unseen God by making his rule visible. It is one thing to say that God, who is invisible, is in control of all things, and quite another to claim or perhaps even demonstrate that a visible agent has similar authority. The authority conveyed to the agent shows both the importance of the agent to God and the confidence God has in the agent to wield that power. At any rate, it is the presupposition that divine prerogatives cannot be shared that leads one to assume that if Jesus is given this authority, then he must be in his very nature divine—or as the language of arguments in theology often goes, that "function implies nature." But this is not a conclusion that the authors of this period drew, at least in any obvious or explicit way. What *is* clearly stated by Paul is that God shares his own name and sovereign rule with Jesus as his supreme agent after the resurrection, and this is not an idea that was felt to be in conflict with monotheism in the texts we have from this period.

And so, given the important roles and status which were attributed to various mediator figures within the context of first-century Judaism, there is no reason to suggest that Paul's presentation of Jesus as God's agent, who occupies a unique role as mediator and has delegated to him the functions and honors of God, would have been felt to be a denial of belief in "one God." The clearest evidence is the highly significant fact that Paul does not feel the need to respond to objections, even hypothetical ones, concerning his exalted view of Christ. Paul's view of the Law provoked controversy, and he spends a great deal of time defending it. If his Christology had shaken one of the other "pillars" of first-century Judaism—the oneness of God—we would surely have heard at least a mention of the fact.[35] That Paul does not defend the exalted status he attributes to Christ suggests that he did not need to. Paul's portrait of Jesus was firmly within the boundaries of first-century Jewish belief in God as one: Jesus offers himself to God "for us" but is never himself envisaged as the recipient of sacrifice. Paul's use of Yahweh texts in connection with Jesus, while distinctive and thought-provoking, would not have represented an attempt to redefine monotheism, and thus should not be read in light of the later developments in Christology to which Paul's writings, in their own way, contributed. In light of all these considerations, I feel compelled to conclude that Paul's portrait of Jesus may only be understood as "Christological monotheism" if one does justice to the fact that, in its original context, it would equally have been an example of "monotheistic Christology."

In conclusion, it is worth drawing attention to Paul's advice regarding sacrifice and idols, issues that *were* regarded as defining boundary markers in Judaism. Paul regards those who have become Christians from among the Gentiles as having turned away from idols to serve the "true and living God" (1 Thess. 1:9) and essentially as no longer being Gentiles (1 Cor. 12:2). Christians should avoid idolatry and food sacrificed to idols, since it is in fact offered to demons. Even though idols themselves have no real power and are not true gods, nevertheless, it is appropriate to shun all contact with them to the extent possible (cf. 1 Cor. 10:7, 14–30). Paul, it seems, sought to walk a narrow line—not between Jewish and non-Jewish perspectives but between two possible implications of monotheism. On the one hand, sacrificial worship is due to one God alone without images, and thus idolatry and sacrifice to idols ought to be avoided. On the other hand, Jewish polemic against idolatry had long emphasized that idols are in fact dead wood and metal, powerless—not real gods—in which case in theory eating food offered to them should not matter. Paul finds a solution which maintains both the traditional Jewish rejection of association with idols and the classic monotheistic denigration of idols as powerless. Paul's recommendation regarding sacrifice and idols falls in line with Jewish monotheism as understood in this period. Indeed, when it comes to the dividing line of sacrificial worship, Paul is every bit as strict as or stricter than his other Jewish contemporaries.[36]

So to return to our starting point, Paul's statement in 1 Corinthians is best understood as adding alongside the Shema an affirmation that God has a unique agent and mediator, who rules the world on his behalf in a way that does not threaten the ultimate lordship of God the Father. This is, after all, what Paul himself says in both Philippians 2:11 and in 1 Corinthians 15:27–28. To Paul, it was obvious that even an apparently universal statement, such as "all things are put in subjection" to Christ had an implicit qualifier, namely, that God is excluded from the things subjected to Christ and is, instead, the one who subjects all things to Christ by his own ultimate sovereignty. In interpreting Paul's writings, the best sense is made of his diverse statements if one understands them to be expressions of a dual conviction as expressed in 1 Corinthians 8:4–6. There is one God, who is above all others, and this God has appointed a single ruler, Jesus the Messiah, to reconcile all things to himself and to rule over God's creation. This conviction of Paul's may perhaps reflect the underlying importance of Adam in Paul's theology: Jesus takes up the role Adam was intended for, as God's viceroy who rules all creation, but who is himself subject to God. Paul's Christology, it is true, incorporates highly exalted claims regarding Jesus, and although these claims are not without Jewish parallels, they are remarkable if nothing else in their concentration. Yet it is hardly surprising that Paul should have applied the most exalted language Judaism had to offer to the person whom Paul was convinced is the Messiah, the promised one, the one through whom God had now accomplished eschatological salvation. Indeed, it would have been surprising if Paul did not *at the very least* offer to Jesus as Messiah all the honors one could legitimately bestow upon a human being within the context of Judaism.[37] However, Jesus is never understood to be "one Lord" in any sense that opposes the ultimate sovereignty of the one God even over Jesus himself, as Paul makes explicit on more than one occasion.

Paul's Christology is thus best understood as monotheistic in the sense that Judaism was monotheistic in this period. Paul was convinced that God was one, above all others and alone worthy to receive sacrificial worship. Although Christians may "call upon the name of the Lord Jesus Christ," using language that was closely connected with the cultic practice of ancient Israel and early Judaism, this language reflects the sort of invocation that was made at times of sacrifice rather than sacrificial practice itself.[38] Jesus reigned with divine authority, bearing God's name, and his name could thus be invoked in seeking divine assistance, even though as a rule Paul continues to pray *to* God *through* or *in the name of* Jesus. The only sacrifices Paul explicitly mentions in his letters are the offering Jesus made to God for us and the offering Christians make to God of their own lives. Jesus is at times thought of as a sacrifice addressed to God, but sacrifice (whether literally or metaphorically) is never said to be offered to Jesus. Paul keeps the ultimate and incontrovertible boundary marker of Jewish monotheism in place. This being so, the exalted status of a mediator figure, even the supremely exalted status of God's unique eschatological mediator, was not felt to detract from this monotheistic commitment. Paul's contemporaries clearly disagreed with him regarding whether Jesus was in fact the promised Messiah. However, there is no evidence that anyone found the statements Paul makes about Jesus controversial in and of themselves. The best explanation for this is the one I have put forward in this chapter: Paul's statements may have been controversial because of who he applied them to, but what he said was in and of itself well within the bounds of what Jewish monotheism could accommodate. Rather than splitting the Shema, Paul presumably regarded himself as upholding it. Just as having a single temple and a single people of God ultimately correlated with the divine oneness, so too the "one Lord" who reigned as God's supreme human representative likewise reinforced rather than detracted from the oneness of God.

4 Monotheism and the Gospel of John

Many readers familiar with recent debates about the development of Christology may find no particular difficulty in accepting the arguments presented in the previous chapter regarding Paul's Christology. Paul, writing in the earliest decades after Easter, was part of the generation that made the first steps in the direction of later Christian thought about Jesus and God, and it is to be expected that his views will not fully express the later Christian understanding of Jesus. In the case of the Gospel of John, however, most readers will assume, or perhaps even be firmly convinced by various pieces of evidence, that we are dealing with a portrait of Jesus that goes beyond the bounds of Jewish monotheism. The Johannine Jesus is accused of blasphemy for "making himself God" even though he is "a mere human being" (John 10:33). Not surprisingly, many scholars take this to be evidence of Christianity's departure from one of the most cherished beliefs of Judaism. Since I have addressed several aspects of this topic elsewhere, I will avoid going over the same ground again.[1] In this chapter, I shall focus on studying John's Gospel in comparison with the writings of some of his Jewish contemporaries to evaluate to what extent John's view of Jesus would have been acceptable within the context of first-century Jewish monotheism.[2] We will find that the evidence points toward a conclusion that may surprise some readers. In terms of Jewish monotheism as it existed in the first century, the evidence suggests that John was completely, undeniably, and without reservations a monotheist.[3]

The Prologue (1:1–18)

The best place to begin is usually at the beginning, and so we may look first of all at the prologue, the hymnlike section found in John 1:1–18. The opening line, "In the beginning was the Word (*Logos*), and the Word was with God, and the Word was God," is obviously of crucial importance for determining the extent to which this Gospel's portrayal of Jesus may rightly be said to be monotheistic. How do such assertions as those made in the prologue compare to what we find in other Jewish sources? In this case, the relevant material is likely to be much more familiar to many readers than some of the other examples mentioned in this book, since there is scarcely any treatment of the Gospel of John that fails to include some mention, if not indeed a full-length treatment, of Philo of Alexandria and his views on the Logos.

In first-century Judaism, many were seeking ways to reconcile the Greek view of God as transcendent, one who would never come into contact with this inferior material world, with the traditions of Israel which maintained that God had not only created the world but acted in human history. For Philo, as for many philosophically minded Jews of the time, God's Word or Logos bridged the gap between God and creation, between the transcendent One and the material realm. In emphasizing this characteristic, Philo describes the Word as "neither uncreated . . . nor created" (*Quis Rerum Divinarum Heres Sit* 206). This may sound like gibberish today, but for Philo, and probably for many others in his time, it made sense in terms of their world view. The Word was "part" of or an "aspect" of God, since it existed within him before coming forth, and yet it could also be spoken of as distinct from God and therefore come into contact with the material world in a way that was felt to be inappropriate for the supreme God.[4] The Word bridged the gap between the transcendent God and the creation. The existence of this "bridge" between God and creation means that although certain religious *practices*, such as cultic worship, distinguished Israel's one God from all other beings, no absolute ontological separation was made, no hard and fast dividing line was drawn, between God and creation. This was certainly true of those who, like Philo, were engaging the teachings of Greek philosophy. It appears, however, to have been more universally true of the Judaism in this period. Recent studies suggest that the doctrine of "creation out of nothing" (in Latin *creatio ex nihilo*) had not yet been formulated in the first century, whether by Jews or Christians.[5] True, they might talk about God creating from "nonbeing," but in this period that was a common way of referring to the primordial chaos that had not yet been brought into a state of "being" through the imposition of order.

This being the case, the Word or Logos itself appears to have been the only boundary marker between God and creation, and the edges were blurred slightly on both sides, since the Word was "neither created nor uncreated," being both the Word of God himself yet also being described as though a separate being. To return to an analogy used earlier, one might say that the boundary between God and creation in first-century Judaism was more like a river than a wall: The exact edges of the boundary were not clearly defined, but the existence of the boundary was not in question.[6] Whatever ambiguity the existence of various personified divine attributes and other such figures may create for us today, first-century Jews affirmed that there was one God who was above all, the creator of all, who was distinguished from other beings in being *alone worthy to receive sacrificial worship* and in being *the supreme ruler of all things* whose will is ultimately always realized.[7] This was not felt to be in contradiction with belief in "intermediary" figures of various types.

Readers ought to consider the paradox the Johannine prologue presents. It says both that the Word was *with* God and that the Word *was* God. This paradox is strikingly similar to what Philo asserts concerning the Word: "neither uncreated nor created." This understanding of the Word is crucial to the role which the Word fulfills, as the one through whom the creation of all things takes place. God's transcendence was so emphasized in non-Jewish Hellenistic thought that it was felt to be inappropriate to suggest that God created directly, or came directly into contact with, the material world. The idea of the Logos thus made it possible to regard God as not only the Creator but also the redeemer who had interacted at various points in history with his chosen people Israel while maintaining his absolute transcendence.

Thus Philo and John both speak of the Word as mediator of creation, as one who is part of the reality of God and yet distinct from and subordinate to God. Both refer to the Word as "God," and yet both emphasize that the Logos is subordinate in some sense to the one true God who is above all. Philo makes this point by referring to the Word as a "second God," while John makes this point by portraying Jesus as calling the Father "the only true God" in John 17:3.[8] For both, then, the Word is an expression of the reality of God himself and yet distinct from and subordinate to God in a way that from our standpoint can only be described as paradoxical. Yet in spite of this paradox, it is clear that if Philo fits our portrait of what a first-century Jewish monotheist might look like (and most would agree that he does), then so also does John; both held that there was one God above all who was uniquely worthy of worship, who created all things through his Word. There is seemingly unambiguous evidence that Philo understood himself to be a monotheist. He writes, "Let us, then, engrave deep in our hearts this as the first and most sacred of commandments, to acknowledge and honor one God who is above all, and let the idea that gods are many never reach the ears of the man whose rule of life is to seek for truth in purity and goodness" (*De Decalogo* 65). This comes from the pen of the same Philo who speaks of the Word as a "second God."[9] It thus becomes clear that both Philo and John—like many other Jews of their time—felt that belief in one God who is above all is compatible with belief in a second figure who reveals and represents God. John's belief was different from Philo's in that he identified this Word with Jesus, but on the question of the oneness of God, it appears that both would have agreed.

"Making Himself [Equal to] God" (John 5 and 10)

A second passage of key importance for understanding Johannine Christology and the way John understood the relationship between Jesus and God is chapter 5 of the Gospel of John. There Jesus is depicted as healing a paralyzed man on the Sabbath. The Jewish authorities object to this, and the Johannine Jesus justifies his action by saying, "My Father is always at work even until this very day, and I too am working" (John 5:17). To understand this response, we need to know that Jewish tradition claimed that God continued to work even on the Sabbath, since it was clear that even on Saturdays someone was busy upholding the universe. This was explained in various ways by Philo and by the later rabbis, but it is clear that already in the first century God was believed to work on the Sabbath, and that this was a prerogative of God alone. For Jesus to claim to do what God alone does was for this reason understood as a claim to be "equal to God."

Reading this passage, we might be tempted to backtrack on the conclusion we reached when looking at the prologue. After all, if John had not abandoned monotheism, what was all this fuss and fighting about? If John had believed in one God, why was it necessary for him to defend himself against the accusation that Jesus had made himself equal to God? In order to understand this, we need to understand that Jesus was understood in terms of the concept of agency discussed in previous chapters. Indeed, personified divine attributes such as God's Word or Wisdom were also depicted as heavenly agents of God. As I

explained earlier, there were certain basic rules or assumptions connected with agency in the ancient world. The most basic of all was
that, in the words of later Jewish rabbis, "The one sent is like the one
who sent him." Or in words that are probably better known to those
of us familiar with the New Testament, "He who receives you receives
me, and he who receives me receives not me but the one who sent me"
(Matt. 10:40). These are words which the Gospels record Jesus as saying
to his apostles, and "apostle" is simply the Greek word for "one who is
sent," an "agent."[10] When someone sent an agent, the agent was given
the full authority of the sender to speak and act on his behalf. If the
agent made an agreement, it was completely binding, as if the person
who sent him had made it in person. Conversely, if someone rejected
an agent, he rejected the one who sent him. The agent was thus functionally *equal* or *equivalent to* the one who sent him, precisely because
he was subordinate and obedient to, and submitted to the will of, him
who sent him.

This helps us to understand what is at issue in John 5. The issue
is not whether there is really only one God—John elsewhere affirms
explicitly that he believes that there is only one true God. Rather, the
debate centers around Jesus' relationship to the one God and whether
or not Jesus has in fact been sent by God. In the Fourth Gospel, Jesus
claims to do what God does. If he is God's appointed agent, then there
is no reason to regard this as illegitimate: It would not be the first time
that God appointed one of his agents to act or speak on his behalf to
proclaim his message and do his works. However, "the Jews" as they
are presented in the Gospel of John do not accept that Jesus has been
appointed by God. They thus accuse him of "*making himself* equal to
God." That is to say, the problem is not "equality with God" in and of
itself, but whether Jesus acts in this way as God's agent. The issue is
whether Jesus has been sent by God and is obedient to God, or whether
he is a rebellious, glory-seeking upstart who claims divine prerogatives
for himself even though God has not in fact sent him. "The Jews" accuse Jesus of *making himself* equal to God—that is to say, they accuse
him of *putting himself* on the level of God, by claiming to do what God
does when he has not in fact been appointed by God. It is for this reason
that they feel that Jesus has committed blasphemy: by making these
claims, he is felt to have insulted God.[11]

How is Jesus portrayed as responding to this charge in John 5? He
adamantly denies it. Note the words which are used: "The Son can do
nothing of himself; he can do only what he sees his Father doing. . . . By
myself I can do nothing. . . . I seek not to please myself but him who

sent me" (John 5:19, 30). The response repeats and negates the two key words used in the accusation: the Greek verb *poiein* means both "to do" and "to make," and thus the reply amounts to an emphatic denial: Jesus does not do/make himself anything. Conversely, Jesus is equally emphatically said to be God's obedient Son and agent. In Mediterranean antiquity, the eldest son was often the principle agent of his father. A son was also expected to learn his father's trade, watching him carefully and learning to imitate his father. The author seems to have this in mind when he uses this type of language to justify the actions and claims of Jesus: Jesus does what God does, and as one who shares in a father-son relationship with God, that is precisely what should be expected. Only if Jesus were a disobedient son would he not do what he sees his father doing. There is thus no problem of monotheism in John 5. The issue is about whether Jesus is *putting himself* on a par with God, seeking his own glory in a way that detracts from the glory and honor due to God alone. John emphasizes that Jesus is in fact God's appointed agent, and because this is the case there is nothing illegitimate about his behavior. He does what God does not as one who is rebelling against the divine authority by setting himself up as a rival to the unique honor and glory of God, but as God's obedient Son and agent whom he sent into the world. Instead of being a debate about monotheism, the belief that God is one serves as the presupposed common ground of both sides of the controversy.

The same applies to John 10:33, where the same sort of language is used: Jesus is accused of *"making himself* God." This would, in the view of his opponents, be blasphemy, precisely because they regard Jesus as a rebellious upstart rather than as an appointed agent. Other figures had at times sought to claim divine prerogatives without being appointed by God: Adam and Eve grasped at equality with God (Gen. 3:4–6), and the king of Babylon was accused of blasphemously exalting himself (cf., e.g., Isa. 47:8–10). Perhaps most relevant for John 10 is the figure of Antiochus IV, known as Antiochus Epiphanes. Antiochus IV was a king of Syria during the late Hellenistic period, when Israel was under Syrian rule. He claimed to be "god manifest," outlawed the observance of the Jewish law, and began a severe persecution of the Jewish people. The dialogue in John 10 is set at the feast of Dedication or Hanukkah, which celebrated the rededication of the temple after it had been desecrated by Antiochus. It is interesting to note that the books of the Maccabees, which describe the desecration of the temple and its subsequent rededication, contain more than a third of all the occurrences of the word "blasphemy" in the LXX, which appears to have been the version that John knew and used. Most striking of all is 2 Maccabees 9:12, where Antiochus is presented as repenting on his death bed and asserting that "no mortal should think that he is *equal to God*," a phrase very reminiscent of the language used in John 10 and in John 5:18. The issue once again is thus whether Jesus is a glory-seeking rebel against God's authority like Antiochus or an obedient agent who does the will of him who sent him. Whether or not there is one God who is uniquely worthy of honor is not at issue; the issue is Jesus' relationship to that one true God.

"I Am" (John 8)

Finally, we may consider the dialogue with Jewish opponents depicted in John chapter 8. This part of John is famous because it presents Jesus as using the phrase "I am" absolutely. Here (and in one or two other places in John), Jesus does not say "I am" followed by a predicate (for example, "I am the good shepherd" or "I am the light of the world"). Rather, he simply says, "I am." Most scholars think that this use of "I am" reflects the occurrence of this phrase in the Septuagint version of Isaiah as a name for God. This in turn appears to have been based on an interpretation of the name "Yahweh" revealed to Moses in Exodus 3:14–15. So we may anticipate the objection that, even if everything noted so far is true, surely when Jesus is presented as saying, "I am" the meaning is "I am Yahweh," and if that is the case then Jesus is clearly claiming to be none other than the God revealed in the Jewish Scriptures and is thus redefining monotheism in a radical way.

This logic would be convincing except for one crucial problem. As C. K. Barrett has rightly pointed out, it is intolerable to suggest that John presents Jesus as saying, "I am Yahweh, the God of the Old Testament, and as such I do exactly what I am told." Yet the Johannine Jesus says in John 8:28, "When you have 'lifted up' [that is to say, 'When you have crucified'] the Son of Man, then you will know that *I am, and that I do nothing of myself, but speak just what the Father has taught me.*" Thus whereas the king of Babylon is accused in Isaiah 47:8 of blasphemously claiming, "I am, and there is no other," Jesus is depicted in John as claiming something very different: "I am, and I do nothing of myself, but only the will of him who sent me." The reference to sending in this context suggests that John's use of "I am" is connected with Jesus being the agent who has been sent by God, and there are Jewish writings from the same time period which can help us to better understand what is going on here.

In the first-century Jewish writing titled the Apocalypse of Abraham, mentioned in the previous chapter, Abraham is described as being granted a visit to heaven. Sent to guide him on his heavenly visit is an angel who identifies himself as Yahoel. The name Yahoel is made up of the two main names for God in the Hebrew Bible, "Yah," or "Yahweh," and "El." The angel thus has the same name as God. This is not because that angel is really God himself or is confused with God. Rather, it is because God has given his name to the angel in order to empower him. This is explicitly stated in the book itself (10:3, 8). In later times, the Samaritans made much the same sort of claims for Moses. In the first century, the early Christians applied these ideas to Jesus. These are all examples of God's agent being given the divine name in order to be empowered for his mission, as discussed in the previous chapter in connection with Philippians 2:6–11. This latter text provides one of the clearest examples of this phenomenon in our period. There we read that "God exalted [Jesus] to the highest place and *gave him the name that is above every name*, that at the name of Jesus every knee should bow, in heaven and on earth and under the earth, and every tongue confess that Jesus Christ is *Lord*, to the glory of God the Father." *Lord* here is thought of as God's name, since the name "Yahweh" was for the most part not actually pronounced by Jews in this period, and in the Septuagint translation they translated the Hebrew name of God with the Greek word for Lord (*kyrios*). This practice has been followed by most modern versions of the Bible, which is why the name "Yahweh," which occurs so frequently throughout the Jewish Scriptures, is not found in them; it has been replaced by LORD (usually in capital letters). Thus in Philippians 2 Jesus is described as being exalted to heaven, to a place second only to God himself, and given God's very own name. This was a way that, in this period of Jewish history, God was believed to honor and empower his agents, and it is a continuation and development of this idea that is found in John. This is particularly clear in John 17:11–12, where Jesus prays for his disciples saying, "Father, protect them by the power of your name—the name you gave me—so that they may be one as we are one."[12] The name "I am" that Jesus bears is the Father's name, and the Father gave it to him because he is the Father's agent. In John's account of the garden of Gethsemane, Jesus speaks the divine name "I am," overpowering those who had come to arrest him (John 18:4–9). He does this, we are told, in order to ensure the release of his followers, thus fulfilling that which he had prayed for in the previous chapter.

Designations for personified divine attributes, such as, for example, "Name" and "Word," were often used interchangeably in first-century Jewish writings. Therefore, in considering these references to Jesus as bearer of the divine name, viewed through the lens of the prologue, it would probably not be far off the mark to suggest that the author of the Fourth Gospel viewed Jesus not just as one who bears God's name, but as God's name "made flesh." That is to say, Jesus and the name are identified to a far greater extent in the Gospel of John than appears to be the case with the angel Yahoel in Apocalypse of Abraham. Nevertheless, the fact that ideas of this sort were widespread in first-century Judaism strongly suggests that John was as much a Jewish monotheist as those of his Jewish contemporaries who made use of similar imagery and motifs.

Hurtado considers the focus not only on the divine name but also on Jesus' name to indicate a significant development within Christianity. Particularly noteworthy is the practice of prayer "in the name of Jesus," which Hurtado believes would have been viewed by Jewish opponents as "an unwarranted and dangerous innovation."[13] Yet while I agree that the attention focused on Jesus in the Gospel of John (as in other early Christian literature) far exceeds the devotion offered to any other figure in Jewish literature, this does not seem a surprising reaction to one who was believed to be God's agent of eschatological redemption. As for parallels, one may note the rabbinic prayers that call upon God to act "for the sake of Abraham" or other patriarchs. Prayer "in the name of" seems to imply the invocation of the name in one's appeal to God; this is something rather different than an appeal *to* the one whose name is invoked. In the Gospel of John it is explicitly denied that the disciples will need to ask Jesus to pray to God on their behalf, which seems to preclude the possibility of prayers addressed directly to the risen Christ as part of the devotional practice of this particular Christian community.[14] Rather, what seems to be envisaged is prayer that mentions the name of Jesus and appeals to his mission or his merits as the reason why God should look favorably on the prayer. That the Messiah might bear the divine name as God's agent, and that his disciples might cry out to God in his name in their hour of need, were ideas for which there was clearly room in early Jewish theology and piety. The fact that these specific practices are not evidenced prior to the rise of early Christianity is best attributed to the fact that, for most if not all of the Jewish groups whose literature we have, the Messiah and the dawn of eschatological salvation were still expected in the future, whereas the early Christians perceived and responded to them as present realities. It is in relation to this point, rather than in relation to the question of God's unity, that early Christianity appears to have stood out as distinctive among the Jewish groups and movements of its time.

Jesus as "God" (20:28)

Before concluding, let us note the application of the designation "God" to Jesus in the Gospel of John. Although there are other instances in the New Testament where Jesus may be referred to in this way, no other New Testament writing does so as deliberately and unambiguously as the Fourth Gospel. Nevertheless, we have already seen that in Jewish writings of this period, the term "god" did not by itself distinguish the one God, who was alone worthy to receive sacrifice, from other figures. In Jewish texts of this period, one still finds "gods" as a way of referring to angels, and thus God Most High is called "God of gods." That Jesus is called *theos*, the Greek word for God, tells us nothing in and of itself about monotheism. However, obviously the designation "God" *can* at times be used to indicate something about monotheism, and so we must look carefully at the relevant texts in this Gospel. Let us first consider potentially relevant instances elsewhere in the Gospel before examining the climactic pronouncement made by Thomas in John 20:28.

The first relevant instance of the use of "God" occurs in John 1:1 and does not strictly refer to the human individual Jesus but to the pre-existent Logos. That the Logos could be called "God" and even a "second God" in Jewish texts from this period has already been shown in the discussion of this verse earlier in this chapter, and I need not repeat these observations here. The next possible reference, in 1:18, most likely refers to the risen and exalted Christ, who is now "in the bosom of the Father," which seems to be another way of saying "alongside the Father" or, in other words, "at the Father's right hand."[15] Modern translations are more or less unanimous in translating John 1:18 as "God the only Son" (NRSV), "God the One and Only" (NIV), "the only begotten God" (NASB), or in some comparable way. The textual evidence for this reading is, however, far more complicated than this agreement of recent translations might suggest. A large number of manuscripts, including some significant early ones, read "only Son." All manuscripts agree on using the typically Johannine designation *monogenēs*, which means "only" or "only one." They differ in adding alongside this word either "God," "Son," or nothing at all. Some assessment of the likelihood of

"God" having been an original feature of this verse in John's Gospel is thus appropriate.

The main reason usually provided for preferring the reading "God" is its early attestation, together with the fact that it is the most difficult reading.[16] However, the argument based on this being the hardest reading has been undermined, rather ironically, by its supporters. After all, it is no good making a convincing case that this is the original form of John 1:18, if one cannot also say what the verse means. For this reason, a number of studies of this verse have argued that *theos* stands in apposition to *monogenēs*, so that the phrase should be translated something like "the only son, who is God."[17] Clement of Alexandria, who is the earliest patristic source to cite the verse in this form, seems to take *monogenēs* and *theos* as separate titles, supporting such arguments.[18] The fact that good sense can be made of this phrase (contrary to the opinions of earlier generations of scholars), and that it was not considered particularly difficult by its patristic audience, implies that there is no reason to regard this text as particularly difficult. This is thus an example of the use of two titles used of Christ elsewhere in John, namely, *monogenēs* and *theos*. This being the case, there is no particular reason why a change should have been made by scribes from "God" to "Son," since there is no real difficulty that needs to be cleared up.

The attestation of two early Alexandrian papyrus manuscripts of the Gospel, known as P[66] and P[75], is frequently given more weight than it deserves. P[75] is indeed a very early text, but it frequently gives a reading which is generally accepted to be inferior, and in a few instances shows signs of conscious additions or alterations having been made.[19] Also significant is the agreement of these two manuscripts in omitting the word *God* in John 5:44, which almost all scholars agree was part of the original text. Beasley-Murray regards this as accidental,[20] but it may equally be the case that the scribes who copied these manuscripts had difficulty referring to the Father as the *only* God, since the Logos can also be spoken of as "God."[21] Also significant is that P[66*] adds the definite article before the word "God" in John 10:33. There are thus indications that the copyists of these manuscripts had a particular theological view which their transcription reflects. Both of these manuscripts preserve inferior readings in abundance, and although their combined weight needs to be taken very seriously, it is not conclusive, as indicated by the general agreement that "only God" is the original reading in the instance just cited (John 5:44).

Margaret Davies has recently put forward a strong case for regarding *monogenēs* as the original reading, the addition of *theos* being an attempt by copyists to make the orthodox doctrine of the church explicit in scripture.[22] This is not to say it reflects the later Arian controversy, which is impossible, given the early attestation of the reading. But even as early as the second century there were other theological debates regarding Jesus, and how the incarnation of the Logos was to be understood. The change, in whichever direction, must have occurred very early, since those church fathers who quote the verse with "God" also show awareness of other readings. And whereas some scholars regard the alteration as having been accidental, perhaps due to a scribal error, the intentional addition of "God" by scribes representing any number of theological agendas would not be surprising.[23]

Davies's point is well taken that the addition of either *God* or *son* is explicable as an attempt to clarify the simpler reading *monogenēs*, whereas it is difficult to understand why either *God* or *son* would be dropped from the text by a scribe.[24] Further, there are many instances of Father/Son and Father/*Monogenēs* type language in John but no example of Father being contrasted with God, much less with "only God." Of course, the evangelist does not appear to have any difficulty with the application of the designation "God" to Christ.[25] However, in view of all the factors and issues discussed, it seems more likely (although by no means certain) that the original reference was simply to the *monogenēs* without designating him as *theos*.[26] True, some might argue that if the original reading was *theos*, this would further highlight the parallel the author draws between verses 1–2 and verse 18.[27] Nevertheless, John also designates God differently in verse 18 than in verse 1 (as "Father" rather than "God"), and the fact that John uses different language in reference to the exalted one does not detract from the fact that it was clearly the incarnate Logos who was so exalted. The author of the prologue reserves the term "Logos" for the preincarnate one and prefers *monogenēs* to designate the incarnate Logos.[28] It would thus be no surprise if the Evangelist used quite different language and terminology here from in verses 1–2, for both literary and theological reasons. In spite of the differences of language, the parallelism remains clear.

The reading in John 1:18 is thus at best textually uncertain, and a strong case can be made that the word "God" did not originally appear there. This does not, at any rate, have any direct impact on this study, as though the use of "God" in reference to Jesus in John 1:18 might somehow lessen the monotheistic character of the work. The only reason for discussing the matter in this context is a concern to discuss what the author of the John's Gospel most likely wrote, and thus to ascertain its most probable original form. The reference to Jesus as "God" in John

20:28 is not disputed and refers to the risen Christ (as would be the case in John 1:18).

It thus remains for us to turn our attention to John 20:28, the only certain reference to the human person of Jesus (rather than the preexistent Word) as "God." It occurs in the context of Thomas's awestruck acclamation before the risen Christ, in which he declares Jesus as "my Lord and my God." From a literary perspective, one might consider the outburst of Thomas, like Peter's suggestion on the Mount of Transfiguration, a spur of the moment utterance that one might not have made had one thought it through more fully. Yet it seems unlikely that the author would have placed on the lips of Thomas here a declaration of faith and devotion that did not accurately express the perspective of his own faith and that of his community. We may thus conclude that the author of this Gospel considered it appropriate to acclaim Jesus as both Lord and God. Both of these could potentially be understood as designations of the one true God. Yet as we saw in the earlier discussions of the designation "Lord," it was possible for other figures serving as God's agents to also bear these titles precisely as designations that were shared by the one true God with his agent. It was also possible for both "god" and "lord" in a broader sense for other figures as well. Once again, we are dealing with titles that were used within the context of Jewish monotheism without provoking controversy. In order to determine whether that is the significance they most likely have in John 20:28, we must engage once again in a comparison with relevant Jewish parallels.

Thus far in this book, I have compared the Gospel of John with other non-Christian Jewish texts from around the same time. It would perhaps be instructive to compare that Gospel to later Jewish-Christian texts as well. Many sources bear witness to the continued existence of groups such as the Ebionites, which retained their Jewish identity and were largely regarded as heretical by the now predominantly Gentile church. One reason they were able to retain their identity as *Jewish* Christians was precisely because their Christology remained subordinationist. How do these later Jewish-Christian texts compare to John's depiction of Jesus? First, under the present heading, we note the explanation that one such source, the Pseudo-Clementine *Recognitions* (2:42), gives regarding the wider use of the title "God": "Therefore the name *God* is applied in three ways: either because he to whom it is given is truly God, or because he is the servant of him who is truly; and for the honor of the sender, that his authority may be full, he that is sent is called by the name of him who sends."[29] In John 10, when Jesus is depicted as defending himself against the accusation of making himself God, it is to the wider use of the designation "gods" that appeal is made.[30] This argument in John 10 must surely be allowed to inform our interpretation of what "God" means in reference to Christ in 20:28. Like later Jewish Christians, the author of the Fourth Gospel can call Jesus "God" yet still refer to the Father as "the only true God" (17:3). In many respects, the language of these later Jewish-Christian writings resembles that of the Gospel of John more closely than that of any other New Testament writing. To quote *Recognitions* 2:48, these later Jewish Christians believed that "the Son . . . has been with the Father from the beginning, through all generations." The group that produced this literature remained alienated from mainstream Judaism because of their belief that Jesus was the Messiah, but their allegiance to only one God was not questioned as far as can be ascertained. They were regarded as heretical by other Christians, however, because of their attempt to preserve their own Jewish identity and because they remained emphatically subordinationist and monotheistic in their Christology rather than assenting to the doctrine of the Trinity as defined by the Council of Nicaea. Within a Jewish-Christian context even in later centuries, then, it was possible to maintain one's allegiance to the one true God and at the same time use language very similar to that found in the Gospel of John. The evidence surveyed in this chapter suggests that this may have been equally true, if not indeed more so, in the time when this Gospel was written.

Conclusion

In highlighting our disagreements with other ways of reading the evidence, we are in danger of seeming to move to the other extreme. It is not my aim to dispute that early Christianity made significant developments that provoked controversy. Rather, it is to clarify what issues did in fact provoke controversy. The claim that Jesus was the Messiah, God's supreme agent, was clearly a sticking point between Christians and non-Christian Jews, and the group whose traditions and experiences are reflected in the Gospel of John are no exception. However, it seems that it was not the things that were said that were in themselves provocative and controversial in the abstract. Rather, what was really at issue was the fact that these things were said *about Jesus*. Similar language applied to an angel, or even to a human being who was universally accepted within Judaism as having been divinely appointed and sent, did not provoke this sort of controversy. This simple fact makes clear that what was at issue was not the idea of the Logos, nor the idea of a divine agent bearing the divine name, but the claim that Jesus was such a figure.

If John had been asked in his day and age, "Are Christians monotheists?" I am convinced that he would have answered with an unreserved "Yes." There are only two clear references in the Fourth Gospel to what today is called "monotheism," and both affirm the oneness of God in rather axiomatic language without defense or explanation (John 5:44, 17:3). If the Johannine Christians had been charged with rejecting monotheism, we would expect the writer to make a more vigorous and explicit defense. But it does not happen. Thus, against Dunn and the majority of New Testament scholars, I am forced to conclude that John would not have been regarded by his Jewish contemporaries as having taken "a step too far" beyond the bounds of what was acceptable within the context of Jewish allegiance to the one true God and him alone.[31]

However, in the centuries after John wrote, other issues arose, and when it was felt necessary to draw a firmer and clearer line between God and creation, it also became necessary to place God's Word clearly on one side or the other. As was mentioned earlier, it appears to have been the development of the doctrine of "creation out of nothing" that was to a large extent responsible for necessitating the clearer definition of what is today considered orthodox Christian belief. I shall have more to say on this topic in the penultimate chapter. Of course, we would love to know what John would have said if he had lived in that time, when it was considered necessary to choose between equality and subordination, between continuity with God and distinction from God. But it is not entirely fair to ask this author questions which only arose quite some time after he had lived and died. John does not give any sort of direct or explicit answer to these questions that were so important to the later church, because in his world view it was still possible to hold that the Word was "neither uncreated nor created" or—in John's own terms—both "God" and "with God." It was only after significant changes in world view had taken place, probably connected with the development of a clear doctrine of creation out of nothing, that it became urgent to sort out exactly where the dividing line between God and creation should be drawn. And so it was that Arius and other non-Nicenes said "between God and the Logos," while Athanasius and the Nicenes said "between the Logos and creation." This does not mean that one must choose between the Gospel of John and later orthodoxy. On the contrary, it could easily be argued that if John had been confronted with these questions, he would have chosen the latter option. For John, Jesus is not the revelation of a lesser god who does not even himself really know the one true God but the revelation of God himself. As I have noted, however, to expect John to answer a question that was only raised later is rather unfair. Yet it was this very question which led to the (re)definition of monotheism by Christians in the trinitarian terms we are familiar with today and by others in monistic terms. Prior to this, there apparently was no problem.[32]

And so in the case of John, as in the case of Paul, the evidence leads us to conclude that John's understanding of God and his portrait of Jesus were firmly within the bounds of early Jewish monotheism. That the boundaries may eventually have changed need not concern us here, since the question we are seeking to answer is whether early Christian views of God and Jesus fit within the understanding of God's oneness that existed within the main stream of Jewish thought in that time. That is the appropriate measuring stick, and based on the evidence surveyed, John seems to measure up nicely as a first-century Jewish-Christian monotheist. If the language of monotheism is appropriately applied at all to authors and other individuals from this period, then it is appropriately applied to John. But even if we find it necessary to look for new terminology that is better suited to the beliefs held by the Jews of this epoch, it remains that same terminology we develop to accurately describe the precise nuances of Jewish devotion to only one God will in all likelihood prove equally applicable to the earliest Christians, including the author or authors of the Fourth Gospel.

5 Monotheism and Worship in the Book of Revelation

There can be no doubting the importance of worship as a theme in the Book of Revelation. Just considering the frequency with which the verb "to worship" (*proskunein*) and its cognates appear, without yet considering any other related terminology or actions, one finds a statistically high occurrence when compared with other New Testament writings. It is found in some form in Revelation 3:9; 4:10; 9:20; 11:1; 13:8, 12, 15; 14:7, 9, 11; 15:4; 16:2; 19:10, 20; and 22:8–9. The spread and frequency of the term alone can be said to give us some initial indication of the theme's importance in the book. Of particular interest in recent times has been the theme of the angelic *refusal* of worship, which is often considered to be highly significant when contrasted with the worship that is offered to the risen, exalted Christ. However, before considering this narrower theme, it is important to have a sense of the overarching theme of worship and its role in the Book of Revelation.

We have already seen the emphasis placed on worship in recent discussions of early Jewish and Christian monotheism. However, as has been noted, the exact *type* of "worship" offered to a figure is also of great importance, since the Greek word for "worship" spans a whole range of activities, from simply bowing before another figure (the primary meaning of this verb) to cultic worship involving liturgy, prayer, and sacrifice. The former could be offered to figures other than God Most High within most streams of Judaism (as discussed in previous chapters); the latter seems to have been reserved exclusively for their

God, and certainly sacrificial worship appears to have been the make-or-break issue for most Jews and Christians. It is thus important to consider the kind of worship offered to Jesus (and other figures) in the Book of Revelation, as well as the titles and actions associated with both the figures in question and their worshippers.

Hurtado, in one of his recent books on the importance of worship in early Christianity, and in particular early Christology, notes this breadth of the verb *proskunein*, and he thus lists a number of other words that normally denote an action or type of worship reserved for the deity alone.[1] Of these, the noun *latreia* ("service") does not occur in Revelation, and the verb *latreuein* occurs only twice: once in 7:15, where it has God as its object, and once in 22:3, where even though there is a reference immediately preceding to the throne of God *and of the Lamb*, it is nevertheless specified that *his* servants worship or serve *him*, which in the context can only be a reference to God. Other verbs Hurtado lists as similarly reserved for cultic and sacrificial worship do not occur at all in Revelation. These terms are, of course, relatively rare in the New Testament, apart from in Hebrews, where the whole argument of the letter revolves around the themes, language, and imagery of cultic worship. However, were Revelation intended to make a Christological point by applying worship-language to Jesus that is normally reserved only for God, then one could only conclude that it misses many opportunities to make this point in a clear and unambiguous manner. Not even the broader verb *proskunein* has Christ as its object in Revelation. We are not told anything more than that others *fell down* before him (1:17, 5:8). And although such worship or reverence is explicitly said to be inappropriate when offered to angels by human beings, this type of worship or bowing down is said to be appropriately offered to Christians in Revelation 3:9.[2] Thus while it is clear that the language and terminology of worship plays an important role in this book, its precise significance and meaning is less immediately apparent, and therefore requires further careful study, which shall be the aim of the rest of this chapter.

Let us begin by looking at who is and is not worshipped in the Book of Revelation and what significance this may have for the author's understanding of the relationship between Jesus and God on the one hand and Jesus and angels or other figures on the other. First and foremost, and most obvious, is the worship offered to God, often designated as "him who sits on the throne." God is the recipient of the majority of the worship mentioned in the book, and of most if not all the worship that is evaluated positively.[3] Chapter 4 marks the beginning of John's heavenly journey, and the first thing he witnesses is a scene of heavenly worship. The description of the worship of God in heaven in 4:1–11 is followed by the description of the Lamb, who is also worthy of praise, honor, glory, and power in 5:1–14. The worship in chapter 5 *includes* the Lamb, in ways we shall consider below, but God continues to be the recipient of worship, and perhaps remains its principal focus. Not much later, in 7:9–17, worship is once again offered to God and the Lamb. Songs of praise and prayers are offered to God in 11:15–19. While songs of thanksgiving are offered for both God and the Lamb and the salvation they have brought to humankind, the one who is always clearly and unambiguously the recipient of both worship and prayer is God, "him who sits on the throne." This is seen again in 15:2–4, where the song that is sung is the song of Moses and of the Lamb but it is addressed to the "Lord God Almighty," who is also the one addressed in the prayers of 16:5–7. In chapter 19, further praise is offered, with God as its recipient. In all such instances of worship, even if the salvation accomplished by the Lamb is the reason and motivating factor for the worship in question, and thus the worship has the Lamb in view as well, nevertheless God is always either the sole or primary recipient of the worship that is offered.[4] Moreover, in all of the instances mentioned thus far, the worship offered constitutes the offering of honor or adulation, and does not incorporate cultic or sacrificial elements.

So are there any examples of cultic or sacrificial imagery being applied to the worship offered to Christ? There are a couple of passages that must be considered. In 14:4 there is a potentially significant metaphor. The chaste remnant of Israel is said to be offered "as first fruits" to God and the Lamb. Here we have the use of an interesting cultic metaphor in reference to both God and the Lamb, with the Lamb being mentioned alongside God precisely as recipient of this offering. However, precisely because it is a metaphorical usage, its significance should not be pressed too far. In context, it need mean no more than that this group represents the first of a larger group to be dedicated to God and the Lamb.[5]

A further cultic image involving both God and the Lamb is to be found in 20:6. Those who participate in the first resurrection are said to be priests of God and of Christ. Since "priests of God" would normally refer to those who offer cultic worship to God in the temple, it is legitimate to ask what the concept of a "priest of Christ" might mean in this context. Here too it seems unlikely that the full cultic overtones and traditional duties of priesthood are in view here. In Revelation 21:22–23, the author's ideal is expressed in terms of a Jerusalem in which no temple is needed, because God and the Lamb are its temple and its light.

To whatever extent the millennial period either foreshadows or symbolizes this eternal ideal, the language of priesthood is best understood in a broader sense, without implying cultic activity or involvement in literal sacrificial worship. That only a broad, metaphorical meaning is in view is most obvious when one considers that those referred to in this way are Christian martyrs. Yet it is said that they *will be* priests, rather than that they *are* priests. In other words, had the author wished to depict the Lamb being offered sacrificial worship, this would have provided a perfect opportunity, since the deaths of the martyrs could have been depicted at this point as sacrifices offered to God and the Lamb. The author, however, chooses not to do so. Also significant is that the only result of their being priests that is explicitly mentioned is that they will reign. The notion of God's people as set apart, a "kingdom of priests," probably provides the background for the language used here. In view of these considerations, the point here is simply that these individuals are set apart for the service of God and Christ during the millennial kingdom.

The sacrificial worship due to God alone is thus not shared in Revelation. What is shared are the divine throne and titles. If at the beginning of the book, "the one seated on the throne" was a designation of God in contrast to the Lamb, by the end of the book the throne is described as being "the throne of God and of the Lamb" (22:1, 3). There is also a clear sharing of the same titles between God and Christ—in particular, "Alpha and Omega" (21:6, 22:13) and "Beginning and End" (21:6, 22:13). This sharing of titles stands within Jewish agency tradition, which transferred titles to an emissary as a way of showing his authority to speak and act for the one who sent him. In one sense, there is no more need to ask what these designations mean when applied to Christ, any more than it would be appropriate to ask what the name of God means when borne by the angel Yahoel or what the designation "the little Yahweh" means when applied to Enoch-Metatron in 3 Enoch. The transfer of name or title singled out the individual in question as the divine agent who represents God's interest fully. When read from our standpoint in history, many find these ideas to be problematic, and indeed, it is for this reason that later rabbis took steps to limit speculation about a chief divine agent. Yet it is important not to read texts like Revelation in light of definitions of monotheism that only arose later.[6] This transfer of designations to God's agent (including ones that normally belong to God alone) is a frequent feature of Jewish and Christian texts from this period.[7] There is thus no need to introduce new terminology such as "divine identity," as Bauckham does. The already-existing language and category of *agency* appears to do justice to the observed phenomena.

It is sometimes asked whether "Beginning and End" when applied to Christ refers to his role in the first creation or in the new creation. But as in other comparable agency texts, the point is neither the same nor a different meaning that the divine name or title carries when borne by the agent, but precisely the fact that these names or titles point away from the agent back to the source of his authority, the one who sent him. The examples from Revelation precisely parallel the transfer of roles and attributes between the sender and the sent, between God and his agent, that one finds elsewhere in early Jewish literature. The language and imagery used is thus well within the bounds of what one might expect to find in a Jewish context as a response to the arrival of God's eschatological redeemer.[8] The fact that the same sharing of throne and sovereignty is explicitly said to extend to Christians as well is not without significance.[9]

Although John prostrates himself before the risen Jesus in 1:17, the first actual occurrence of the verb *proskuneō* is found in 3:9, where it is before Christians that those of the "synagogue of Satan" will worship. When taken together with the points made previously, it becomes clear that neither sharing the throne nor receiving worship was something this author reserved exclusively for God alone, or even exclusively for God and Christ. It is therefore unlikely that worship is used in Revelation to make a subtle Christological point. The act of worship or prostration before another is a sign of submission, expressing recognition of the status of the other as worthy of honor. Presumably the Christians who are in view had had contacts with a synagogue which had been felt by them to be dishonoring. Here the risen Christ is depicted promising to the church that their opponents will eventually show them honor and acknowledge that they were right.

After overcoming through death and showing himself worthy to open the scroll, the Lamb is said to stand in the midst of the throne, and to receive worship in the form of prostration and song (5:6–14). The most striking point in this passage for our purposes is probably the mention of the elders holding not only harps, but also bowls of incense "which are the prayers of the saints."[10] The prayers/incense mentioned here, while clearly part of the paraphernalia of worship employed in the Lamb's presence, are nowhere said to be offered directly to the Lamb. It is thus possible that the author assumed such prayers to be either offered to God in thanksgiving for Christ, or offered to God *through* Christ, just as the elders appear to be mediators of the prayers in bringing and presenting them before God and the Lamb. The description in 8:3–4 of an angel offering these prayers/incense before *God*, with no mention of the Lamb, can be regarded as confirming this reading.[11]

It is often suggested that the heavenly worship that is described in Revelation is patterned on the worship services of the early Christian communities. If this is true, then the description of the prayers of the saints as incense may indicate a conviction that the worship of the Christian churches in some way replaces the cultus of the Jerusalem temple. The author could presumably also be making the same point over against the worship in the synagogues, as some of the hymns in Revelation bear striking resemblance to those used in the synagogue liturgy in later times. This may, however, simply be due to the fact that the worship of the Christian churches was indebted to Jewish models, without any further polemical interest intended.

The inclusion of God's appointed representative alongside God as recipient of praise is noteworthy, but it is neither unique nor without precedent.[12] Such a development was foreseen to a certain extent, and was perhaps even to be expected as a response to the appearance of God's agent in the realization of his eschatological salvation.[13] Thus far we have observed no acts of worship that were normally reserved for God alone being unambiguously transferred to the Lamb. None of the features we have considered in this study appear inappropriate within the boundaries of early Jewish monotheism as attested in the extant literature from this period.[14] And so the depiction of Christ in the Book of Revelation represents a development *within* the context of Jewish monotheism rather than a development *away from* Jewish devotion to only one God.

We must now turn to two additional examples of worship in the Book of Revelation, the illegitimate worship of the beast and of an angelic figure. These negative examples are foils which are presumably intended to bring out the significance of that worship which the author regards as legitimate. We may begin with the worship of the beast, which presumably has in view the situation that arose wherein Christians were put under great pressure to offer sacrifice to the emperor and/or pagan gods (cf. 12:8,15–17). This worship is one reason for the divine judgment that comes upon the empire and upon humankind, as is described later in Revelation. While the enigmatic character of some of the riddles associated with this worship may hinder any attempt to offer a detailed interpretation, what is quite unambiguously clear is that the heavenly worship of God and the Lamb is evaluated positively while the earthly worship of the beast is a dark counterfoil thereto. The contrast is certainly intentional. Of particular interest is the way this evidence from Revelation suggests that the worship of Christ was not patterned on non-Jewish models.[15] On the contrary, in this very Jewish work, one finds an outright rejection of the Greco-Roman cultus side by side with an incorporation of Jesus into the heavenly worship (which presumably in turn reflects his incorporation into the earthly worship of the Christian Church). This confirms (if there was ever any doubt) that the worship of the Lamb is not added alongside the worship of Israel's only God to form a sort of Christian pantheon. Rather, he is allowed to share God's throne, titles, and other prerogatives in a manner familiar from other Jewish literature that uses the agency model to attribute such things to other figures in a similar way.

The depiction of the worship of the beast as blasphemous also shows the strength of Jewish and Christian sensibilities as regards the *cultic* (i.e., sacrificial) worship of another figure. Persecutions on the part of the Roman authorities against Christians in the centuries that followed regularly focused on worship of this sort, and it was here that the martyrs took their stand. No other god or figure was to receive this worship. This sensibility continued long after there ceased to be a sacrificial cult offered to their own God in the Jerusalem temple. This provides further confirmation that Hurtado, Bauckham, and others are right to regard worship as the (or at least the most important) "dividing line" that defined Jewish monotheism in this period. However, it seems to have been specifically the issue of sacrificial worship, which suggests that other types of "worship" will not have functioned to make a Christological point about the divinity of Christ. As the death of Christ was regarded as the sacrificial worship par excellence that was offered to God, there was no real way that he could be portrayed as both the one who offers such sacrificial worship, and at the same time the recipient thereof. Thus while important in understanding monotheism in this period, worship is unlikely to provide the key to unraveling the development of early Christology into later trinitarianism. It must also be emphasized that early Jewish sensibilities regarding worship in the broader sense appear to have depended to a large extent on the question of *whom* one honored in this way. To show reverence and obeisance before God's agent of salvation could often be appropriate; to show the same reverence to a pagan king who did not honor God or to a god other than the one true God was unacceptable and blasphemous.[16]

What, then, of the worship offered to and rejected by the angelic figure? In two verses, 19:10 and 22:9, we find the seer prostrating himself before the angel to worship him. This feature of the Book of Revelation has been the subject of a significant amount of scholarly attention in recent times.[17] It is frequently thought that the author's coupling of this motif with his portrait of the worship of Jesus makes a Christological point, namely, that Jesus is now placed on the divine side of the dividing line between God and creation, so that he receives the worship that was previously reserved only for God himself. In view of the evidence surveyed, this appears to be an over-interpretation of the evidence. The worship/prostration offered to Jesus was not without parallel within Judaism, and most Jews are unlikely to have found it objectionable *in and of itself*.[18] What, then, is the meaning of the angelic refusal of worship? If such prostration before another figure was often acceptable and is permitted in Revelation itself as an appropriate action toward Christians (3:9), then the point is presumably not about worship per se but relates specifically to the significance of the worship of an angelic figure by a human being.

Before proceeding, it is necessary to ask whether there is any significance in the fact that the angelic refusal of worship is *repeated*. Rather than representing an emphasis through repetition on this particular worship-related point, the repetition is part of a larger structural and linguistic parallelism between two passages, Revelation 17:1–19:10 and 21:9–22:9, as Aune has clearly demonstrated.[19] The repetition of this particular element may therefore be little more than a way for the author to draw attention to the parallel between these two passages, rather than being intended to draw attention to the angelic refusal of worship for its own sake.

In the literature of this period, there are a number of places where the view is expressed that angels and similar heavenly figures are antagonistic to humans. Here we must avoid seeking to relate Revelation to significantly later writings, such as the rabbinic literature and the Life of Adam and Eve. Although these works provide some of the most interesting parallels and points of comparison, they are too distant temporally from the time when Revelation was written for it to be legitimate to appeal to them in our search for knowledge of the background against which Revelation was written.[20] Nevertheless, the idea of some form of angelic antagonism toward humans is attested clearly in the New Testament (including but not limited to the Book of Revelation itself) and the Dead Sea Scrolls.[21] There is thus no need to depend on or appeal to the evidence of later works, which present these ideas in a much more elaborate form and presumably represent further developments along the same trajectory as the Book of Revelation.

In the Gnostic and mystical writings of subsequent centuries, the antagonism of celestial forces usually comes to expression when one seeks to ascend past the heavenly powers. By way of contrast, as Aune has rightly noted, the cosmology of a multitiered heaven that is typical of such ascent traditions is entirely absent from Revelation.[22] There are no references to multiple heavens, nor to anything that would indicate that the existence of such is presupposed. Nevertheless, as in works that presuppose the Ptolemaic cosmology, Revelation regards heaven not as the dwelling place of God and his allies alone, but also of antagonistic celestial powers. Thus it is that Satan is eventually "cast *down* to the earth" after having been involved in warfare in heaven (cf. Revelation 12:7–13). The author appears to share the apocalyptic view that the struggles of the people of God on earth are parallels to heavenly struggles that are taking place. The role of angels in the Book of Revelation cannot be underestimated. They serve throughout as those who inflict God's judgment upon the earth, and beginning with chapter 12 (although hints had already been given in 2:9, 13, 24; 3:9, with their references to Satan) it becomes increasingly clear that the struggle of the church is not just between Christians and earthly authorities but has a spiritual, celestial dimension as well. In this context, the relationship between humans and angels would have been important. In Revelation, we find the following uses of worship, and it will soon become apparent how these may relate to the issue of the relationship between angels and humankind:

1. Christians will be worshipped by their human opponents (3:9).
2. God and the Lamb are worshipped by humans and angels (chaps. 4–5).
3. Disobedient humans worship the beast and/or its image (13:8, 15).
4. Humans like John should not worship angels because they are their fellow servants of God (19:10, 22:9).

The meaning of the angelic refusal of worship probably has little to do with distinguishing Christ from angels or with making a subtle point concerning monotheism and Christology. Rather, the refusal of worship has to do with the point the angel himself is presented as making: Angels are fellow servants of God together with Christians, and thus Christians are to regard themselves as equal to them. In the context of persecution in which the book was written, the whole world appeared to be against the Christians, and they believed themselves to be the targets of an onslaught by malevolent heavenly beings. In this context, the emphasis placed on the dignity and equality of humans in God's creation presumably would have offered considerable encouragement. Rather than having to live in subjection to the whims and attacks of antagonistic celestial forces, Christians were encouraged to believe that God and Christ are rulers over the creation. This is a point that is made in other early Christian literature as well, in particular Colossians. Here in Revelation it is further emphasized that humans are not to be considered inferior to angels. The worship offered to Christ also would have reinforced this point: In heaven, seated on the throne, a throne which Christians who overcome will share, the recipient of the worship of all creation (both human and angelic) is a human being, Jesus Christ. This is presumably one of the key points that the author wished to make through his multifaceted use of a multiplicity of worship-related images in Revelation. These points were certainly new and distinctive emphases of Christianity. Their distinctive claims were made, however, in a way that did not depart in any obvious or significant way from the Jewish understanding of and devotion to one God alone.

In the next chapter, we shall jump ahead several centuries from the New Testament age to the rabbinic literature in an attempt to determine when the controversy between Jews and Christians over monotheism does in fact begin. But before proceeding, it is worth noting that even in the second century, when Justin Martyr (to take one convenient example) clearly regarded Jesus as the incarnation of the preexistent, personal Logos, he does not argue against Jewish accusations that he (and others like him) had denied or abandoned monotheism.[23] In his *Dialogue with Trypho the Jew*, he argues whether Jesus was the Messiah, whether the Messiah would be a preexistent figure, and whether the preexistent Logos would become a human being and suffer, but the idea that there is such a Logos is not in and of itself controversial. And so it seems that the agreement between Jews and Christians over monotheism lasted beyond the New Testament era. How far beyond? That is the question we address in the next chapter.

6 Two Powers Heresy:
Rethinking (and Redating) the Parting of Ways between Jewish and Christian Monotheism

Our understanding of early Judaism and its relationship to Christianity has been significantly advanced by Alan Segal's famous work on the "two powers heresy."[1] His research demonstrated that belief in two heavenly powers was considered an intolerable heresy by the rabbis and that Christians were among those indicted.[2] Furthermore, Segal argued that the two powers debate could be traced back to the first century, as evidenced by certain Christological passages of the New Testament and by Philo's writings.[3] Thus, according to Segal, the two powers controversy provided the context for the New Testament and, conversely, these writings shaped rabbinic reports about those who claim "there are two powers in heaven."

Segal's study has widely influenced both Jewish and Christian scholarship.[4] Among its contributions, the study firmly placed early Christological development and controversy in a *Jewish* setting. It also took a critical approach to the dating and redaction of rabbinic literature. However, Segal's study is not without shortcomings. For example, Segal appears to maintain that there was a clear "orthodoxy" in first-century Judaism, whereas the existence of a clearly recognizable orthodoxy during this period is much debated.[5] Furthermore, his conclusions regarding the historicity of certain stories in the rabbinic corpus are open to challenge. In this chapter, therefore, I shall reassess the evidence regarding this topic in the rabbinic literature and its relationship to earliest Christianity and its environment.

Segal hints at three possible ways of relating the "two powers" debate to first-century Judaism. First, we have the interpretation Segal himself appears to favor, stressing *continuity* or *consistent condemnation*.[6] On this interpretation of the evidence, the belief that there were two powers in heaven was condemned as a heresy in rabbinic literature, just as the same belief was condemned as a heresy in first-century Judaism. This view maintains that there was continuity in belief (it was the same belief over the centuries) and continuity in rabbinic condemnation (it was not accepted at any time). A second possible way of conceptualizing the matter can be called *retrospective* condemnation. That is, certain first-century Jewish beliefs were later classified as "two powers heresy" and retrospectively condemned in rabbinic literature.[7] Here we have continuity in belief (the same belief) but not in condemnation (earlier the belief in question was accepted, or at the very least tolerated, whereas later it was not). A third explanation emphasizes *development*, that is, particular first-century Jewish beliefs evolved into a form which became intolerable for the rabbis.[8] In this view, there is only partial continuity of belief (it changed over time), and there is discontinuity regarding condemnation (only the later form was rejected).

Segal's study has demonstrated that a similarity exists between some first-century exegesis (like Philo's) and later "two powers" discussions in the rabbinic literature. However, he has not provided corroborating evidence for his overall conclusion in two ways. First, Segal has not provided evidence that Philo, for example, was regarded by his Jewish contemporaries as a heretic, which Segal's work might lead us to expect. This suggests that a retrospective explanation may be possible. Second, Segal has not demonstrated that specific first-century beliefs were identical with those later condemned, which opens the way for a developmental explanation. Thus I believe there are grounds for questioning whether or not Christological passages in the New Testament ought to be read in light of the two powers heresy of rabbinic Judaism. Although various forms of "two powers" conceptuality may have been present in first-century Christian and Jewish thought, I will argue that there is no evidence they were identified as heretical during that century.

Methodology and Dating

The last couple of decades of study of rabbinic literature can almost be described as a revolution, as critical methodology developed in the field of New Testament studies and other scholarly disciplines have been applied to the relevant source material. Thus recent critical studies have eclipsed earlier rabbinic scholarship, which often took materials separated by many centuries to form a monolithic entity called "Judaism."[9] However, the fact that this revolution has taken place so recently means that there is still uncertainty in many areas, particularly with respect to the dating of documents. On questions of dating rabbinic material, New Testament scholars can for the most part do little more than accept the results reached by scholars in the field of rabbinic studies, and where necessary to note differences of opinion.

Perhaps even more important for our purposes, however, is the question of the relationship between (1) the date assigned to a particular rabbinic document and (2) the date of the rabbis who appear in that work. It has long been axiomatic in New Testament scholarship that written documents tell us about the *Sitz im Leben* of the authors and only secondarily—and through critical study—about any earlier period described in those works. This axiom, increasingly recognized and accepted by scholars engaged in academic study of the rabbinic literature, informs this book's approach to rabbinic material. So, for example, later documents which attribute to earlier rabbis views that are nowhere attested in earlier writings must be treated with some degree of skepticism.[10]

Although I do not wish to exclude potentially valuable information from any quarter, this study limits itself to Jewish literature through about 600 CE, when the Babylonian Talmud reached closure.[11] Even though it may be at least theoretically possible that later documents can tell us something about first-century Jewish-Christian relations, in any other discipline the use of documents dating from centuries after the time being studied would be considered methodologically suspect. This ought to be true of rabbinic studies as well.[12] Although this study has as its primary aim to illuminate first-century Jewish-Christian theology in relation to two powers belief, I shall nonetheless investigate later traditions to determine what, if anything, can be firmly traced to the first century.

The Start of the Controversy

Before proceeding, I should note two further points about the rabbinic discussions of two powers and the first century. First, there are no references within rabbinic literature linking two powers with any of the first-century rabbis.[13] Second, the Babylonian Talmud and 3 Enoch in their present form date the origin of the two powers controversy to the early second century. Although we shall see that there are reasons to question the historical reliability of this tradition, it is noteworthy that no attempt was made by rabbinic sources to link the two powers controversy to events or persons of the first century, in the time of Jesus, Philo, Paul, and John.

MISHNAH AND TOSEFTA

We may now turn to the earliest rabbinic sources on this subject, namely, the passages in the Mishnah and Tosefta which are thought to contain allusions to two powers. It is noteworthy that the phrase itself never appears in these writings, a fact which is given more significance when one considers that the Tosefta contains several references to Christians as *minim* (heretics).[14] The lack of explicit reference to two powers, therefore, cannot be explained as a lack of interest in Christianity, since the rabbis who composed the Tosefta took the trouble to polemicize against Christians. So if Christian belief in "two powers in heaven" was an issue at that time, it is quite surprising that the Mishnah and the Tosefta do not address the issue in those terms.

Nevertheless, there are several passages from the Mishnah and the Tosefta which Segal takes to allude to the two powers heresy, and these must be examined. The first passage refers to certain heretics who say there are "many ruling powers in heaven":

> M. Sanhedrin 4:5: Therefore but a single man was created in the world . . . that none should say to his fellow, "My father was greater than your father"; also that the heretics should not say, "There are many ruling powers in heaven."

The phrase used in this Mishnaic passage is not "two powers" but "many powers," which suggests a distinct set of beliefs.[15] While this brief pericope leaves a number of questions unanswered, its meaning appears to be clear enough: If numerous human beings had been created, people might have concluded that this was evidence of several creators. The "many powers" sounds suspiciously like polytheism, and it may be that there were Jews (non-Jews cannot be in mind because of the use of *minim*) who believed that it was not God but the angels who created the world. Justin Martyr refers to Jews who hold such a belief, calling it "heresy."[16] The evidence from Justin suggests that one could reject creation by angels and yet believe in the Logos (or a similar supreme mediator or personified divine attribute). It is the former sort of belief which the rabbis appear to refer to as "*many* powers," whereas it is the latter which eventually developed into or came to be regarded as heretical belief in "*two* powers." The two are not entirely unrelated, but neither are they simply to be identified.

The view that lesser beings created the world was a key element in certain streams of Hellenistic Judaism and in Gnosticism, both of which were influenced by contemporary Platonism. At least some Jews in the Hellenistic age believed that angels had created the world, while the Gnostics posited the existence of a demiurge, distinct from the high God, who created the (evil) world, often with helpers.[17] The Mishnah's argument makes sense as a response to such views. It argues from the biblical account that only one human being was created to be the origin of all human kind, which in turn implies that there was one creator, not many.[18] This is similar to the argument that, just as there is one temple and one nation chosen by God, so also there is only one true God.[19] Therefore, *m. Sanh.* 4:5 does not appear to identify the sort of Logos doctrine held by Philo and the early Christians as heretical; it is more likely aimed at beliefs which were moving in a Gnostic direction.[20] Beliefs of this sort were an issue for Christians in the second century, and may well have been for Jews as well.[21] Although we are probably dealing with something distinct from "two powers" in this passage, it is possible that this early use of "powers" language provided the basis for the use of "two powers" later on. If so, the designation may have been used to stigmatize those who held such beliefs as little better than those who had polytheistic or Gnostic leanings.

Next we shall look at three passages from the Mishnah also thought by Segal to refer to the two powers heresy. These warnings focus on what is acceptable and unacceptable prayer:

> *M. Berakot* 5:3: He who says [in a prayer]: "Even to a bird's nest do your mercies extend" or "May your name be remembered for the good" or "We give thanks, we give thanks"—is to be silenced.

> *M. Megillah* 4:9: He who says "May the good bless you"—this is the manner of sectarianism.

> *M. Ber.* 9:5: Man is bound to bless (God) for the evil even as he blesses (God) for the good.

The meaning of the first prayer concerning "a bird's nest" is obscure, as it was to the later rabbis who discuss it in *b. Berakot* 33b and *b. Meg.* 25a.[22] The latter two prayers are associated with "two powers" in the Babylonian Talmud, but this may very well represent an attempt either to understand an obscure decision by earlier rabbis, or to make an earlier decision relevant to the issues of their day. As it stands, the prayers which thank God for the good but not for the evil appear to imply an opposing dualism or Gnosticism: God is to be thanked for the good, but another power is to be blamed for the evil. The opponents in mind here are unlikely to be either early Christians or Jews with beliefs similar to those of Philo.

In the first prayer, we find the repetition of "We give thanks." It was easy for later rabbis to associate this with "two powers," since it was the repetition of the name of God in the Hebrew Scriptures that "two powers heretics" often appealed to in support of their beliefs.[23] However, as Segal himself acknowledges, "The amoraic traditions concerning the prayer do not clarify the heresy. Although they assume that such prayers are to be silenced because they manifest 'two powers in heaven,' they do not explain how. We may suspect that they themselves were guessing. We must also be prepared to allow that the tannaim in their day were worried by different phenomenon [*sic*] from the amoraim."[24]

In addition, Segal notes that the repetition of the words in the synagogue liturgy is unlikely to have been the real problem, since the rabbis came to require a repetition. He suggests that it may be the Eucharistic prayers of Christians which are in view, since the Didache includes a double thanksgiving as part of the Eucharistic service (Did 9:2–3).[25] This is highly speculative, but even if it is correct, there is no indication that the problem was prayer which mentioned a second power. The Didache has only prayer to the Father, giving thanks for Jesus. The glory clearly goes to the one God for Jesus, without any hint of two powers. Alternatively, Gruenwald suggests that the problem may have been adding one's own prayer alongside those which were part of the official liturgy. Introducing a personally composed prayer with the same language as the official liturgy (*modim*, "we give thanks") would be in danger of claiming official status.[26] In view of the uncertainty about what was being objected to in *m. Ber.* 5:3, it seems prudent not to assume that the repetition of "We give thanks" is a reference to two powers unless further evidence is forthcoming.

Finally, we turn our attention to a passage from the Tosefta, probably composed in the decades immediately after the completion of the Mishnah. Here a reference is made to *minim* who believe, or who might reach the conclusion, that God had a partner in creation, specifically *Adam*:[27]

> *T. Sanh.* 8:7: Our rabbis taught: Adam was created on the eve of the Sabbath. And why? So that the heretics could not say: The Holy One, blessed be He, had a partner in his work (of creation).

We know from a number of Jewish sources that, in some circles at least, Adam was believed to have been created as a great being. Philo even distinguished between a heavenly and earthly Adam, but it is unlikely that his sort of exegesis is the object of this polemic. Philo interpreted Genesis 1 as the creation of heavenly things, and thus for him the heavenly Adam, identified with the Logos, did in fact have a role in the creation of the earthly realm. Yet *t. Sanh.* 8:7 does not seem to address this type of exegesis.[28]

The saying is perhaps best interpreted as a response to the traditions which glorify Adam and almost turn him into a divine being. However, the polemic is not against the idea that Adam was created as a splendorous being per se, but against the idea that he was God's partner in creation. Thus the rabbis were placing a limit on the exalted status of Adam in order to check unbridled speculation: Adam, however glorious and exalted, did not create. It must be pointed out that there is nothing in this passage to indicate that any group actually held the views described here. It is possible that the rabbis are *hypothetically* addressing what heretics *might have said* if Adam had not been created on the sixth day. Nevertheless, if the *t. Sanh.* 8:7 tradition *is* related to the issue of two powers—and this is far from clear that this is the case—then it is at best one of the first indicators that two powers belief is becoming problematic. Thus even if for the sake of argument we grant that *t. Sanh.* 8:7 is related to the two powers controversy, this does not provide grounds for dating the controversy earlier than immediately prior to the composition of the Tosefta, in the first half of the third century CE. In all likelihood, however, the beginnings of the controversy are to be dated even later.

BABYLONIAN TALMUD

Since the Mishnah and Tosefta show no clear signs of the "two powers" controversy, it is likely that the controversy only arose after the formation of these documents. Nonetheless, later rabbinic writings trace the origins of the controversy to the early second century CE. I will therefore discuss two key passages from the Babylonian Talmud which mention rabbis from this period. The first passage reads:

b. Hagigah 14a. One passage says: *His throne was fiery flames* (Dan 7:9)
and another passage says: *Until thrones were placed; and One that was
ancient of days did sit*—there is no contradiction; One (throne) for Him
and one for David: this is the view of R. Akiba. Said R. Yosi the Galilean
to him: Akiba, how long will you profane the Shekinah? Rather, one for
justice and one for mercy. Did he accept (this explanation) from him, or
did he not accept it? Come and hear: One for justice and one for mercy;
this is the view of R. Akiba.

Segal recognizes that "no one would suggest that these are Akiba's
actual words." He also acknowledges that, even if Akiba did hold to beliefs such as those represented here, the portrait of him recanting his
earlier view may well be an attempt to bring him into line with later
"orthodoxy."[29] Thus even if Akiba maintained some form of belief in
"two powers," this still would not demonstrate that his belief would
have been regarded as objectionable *in his time*. Further, it is not entirely clear that this story, if it does represent an authentic tradition
about Akiba, was originally about two powers. In its present position
within the Babylonian Talmud, this story is situated in the context of
a discussion of subjects related to two powers. However, if the dialogue
between R. Akiba and R. Yosi is taken on its own, the issue may simply be whether any human figure—even a unique human figure like the
Messiah—is worthy to sit alongside God in heaven.[30] Such a discussion
presupposes belief in the uniqueness of God but does not necessarily
deny or challenge it, although it does begin to question the status attributed to exalted human beings in earlier Jewish literature.

One should compare this passage with the tradition concerning the
trial of Jesus before the Sanhedrin recorded in the Synoptic Gospels,
in which the high priest is depicted as condemning Jesus to death for
"blasphemy" because he asserted that they will see the Son of Man
(with whom he implicitly identifies himself) seated at God's right hand.
Here too there is no reason to think that Jesus was being accused of
abandoning monotheism.[31] Rather, he was felt to have claimed for himself a status which was too high for a human being, or at least for one
who was rejected by the leaders and condemned to death.[32] Akiba was
remembered for having identified Bar Kochba as the Messiah, and this
may have been part of the difficulty in the rabbinic passage: to have
made messianic claims for someone who was put to death by the Romans may have been what was really the sticking point.[33] On the other
hand, to make extravagant claims for any human being in the present
day may have met with resistance. There is probably a psychological aspect to this issue which is worthy of further investigation. It certainly

seems that people are often willing to make assertions concerning "canonical" heroes and figures of the ancient past that they would be unwilling to make or accept concerning one of their contemporaries. At any rate, the most that can be said with certainty is that to make grandiose claims for a failed messiah was felt to be "blasphemy" or "profaning the Shekinah" in the sense of "insulting to God."[34] There is nothing which necessitates the conclusion that this tradition was originally connected with the "two powers" heresy or involved a debate about monotheism itself.[35]

The second passage from the Babylonian Talmud is the most famous "two powers" tradition. It concerns the apostasy of R. Elisha ben Abuya, often referred to as "Aher" (meaning "other") in rabbinic tradition. The story is preserved in *b. Hag.* 15a and (in a different form) in 3 Enoch 16. Regarding *b. Hag.* 15a, Segal acknowledges that the "tradition is a late addition to the Babylonian Talmud."[36] This means that we are dealing with a gap of more than three centuries between the time Aher lived and the writing of this story in the Talmud. The authenticity of the tradition is thereby thrown into serious question. In a similar vein, P. Alexander writes, in reference to the attribution of 3 Enoch to R. Ishmael (d. 132 CE), that "there can be no question of accepting this attribution at face value; the work is a pseudepigraphon and Ishmael is simply the authority the author or redactor of 3 Enoch wished to claim."[37] He dates 3 Enoch to the fifth–sixth century CE while acknowledging that a later date is not impossible.[38] In addition, chapter 16, which contains the tradition concerning Aher's apostasy, shows signs of being an interpolation into 3 Enoch and so can be dated even later.[39]

The lack of mention of "two powers" in the Mishnah is thus highlighted by the fact that this important rabbi-turned-heretic is not associated with this heresy until hundreds of years after his apostasy is said to have taken place. The connection between Aher and the specific heresy of two powers in heaven is thus problematic, and there is no way of knowing how early or late his name first became associated with this particular controversy. Even if the historical Elisha ben Abuya did hold views which were *later* censured, this still does not provide evidence that, *in his own day and age* they would have been regarded as unacceptable.[40] It would therefore be ill advised to accept this tradition as evidence of a controversy which involved these near-contemporaries of the New Testament authors. The story is explicable in terms of the tendency to attribute later heresies to earlier figures who were already regarded as heretics and to attribute responses to those heresies to earlier, well-known, authoritative sources. Thus in Gruenwald's words, "It is quite likely that the rabbis found in 'Elish'a ben 'Avuyah a peg on which they hung a variety of heretical views."[41]

The evidence surveyed thus far gives no support for dating the origins of the controversy even to the second century. It is of course possible that the controversy did arise in the second century but had not yet had sufficient impact to leave any clear or explicit trace in the traditions and literature from that period. However, in the absence of proof, any suggestion that the two powers controversy was already underway in the second century must remain at best hypothetical. Of course, conversely, the absence of evidence for the existence of the heresy in the period surveyed so far does not prove that it did not yet exist. However, in view of the clear polemic against two powers in later writings, the complete absence of such polemic in earlier writings at least strongly suggests the possibility that two powers only became an issue, for whatever reason, in the period after these documents were put in their present form.

MIDRASHIM

We find the first explicit reference to "two powers" in the so-called Tannaitic Midrashim, which date from the period after the composition of the Mishnah and Tosefta. The earliest reference is probably *Sifre Deuteronomy* 379, which seems to have Gnosticism in mind.[42] When the rabbis describe "two powers" as antagonistic, Gnosticism is indicated; when the "two powers" are complementary, it is something else.[43] With this distinction in mind, *Sifre Deuteronomy* 379 seems to be combating a Gnostic version of two powers belief because it argues against the view that one power is responsible for life and another power for death.[44] The reference in *Mekhilta de-R. Ishmael* is also probably aimed at Gnosticism of some form.[45] The point which it attributes to R. Nathan (c. 135–170)—that when the Holy One claimed, "I am the Lord thy God," no one protested—suggests an opposition between the two powers and recalls the Gnostic stories of the God of the Jews claiming to be the only God when he was in fact ignorant of the true God.[46] The earliest use of the term "two powers" thus appears to be as a reference to Gnosticism. This is exactly the opposite of the conclusion reached by Segal.[47] The terminology first appears in writings of the third century and is initially used in reference to the idea of two opposing or dualistic powers rather than in reference to ideas like those attested in Philo, the Enochic literature, and Early Christianity, although it is not long before the same terminology comes to be applied to the latter concepts as well.

The Third-Century Context

This reevaluation of the tradition history of the two powers material, and of the controversies which formed them, may explain the continuity which exists between the exegesis of the "two powers heretics" and earlier traditions and views. Scholars have long noted that writers like Philo share some views in common with Gnosticism, probably because of their common Platonic heritage rather than through direct influence.[48] It is likely that other Platonizing Jews were responsible for developing Gnosticism, and thus they may have been influenced either by Philo's own writings, or by the Hellenistic Jewish traditions which influenced Philo. Similarly Neusner has noted that although there is no clear evidence that the authors of the Mishnah were aware of and interacting with Gnosticism, they come down firmly on matters which also interested the Gnostics, but with the opposite conclusions.[49] The designation "two powers" may thus have originally been applied to a heresy (and that there were Jewish Gnostics seems very likely) with which the rabbis had perhaps already begun to interact in the second century without calling it by that specific name.[50] Not long after the terminology was coined, ideas about exalted angels, patriarchs, and similar mediator figures came to be called by the same name and tarred with the same brush.

Yet it is not surprising that Gnosticism should have first raised problems for Jewish monotheism, before mediator figures aligned with the divine plan and purpose. Gnosticism creates a crisis, not because it allows for emanations from God but because it offers an opposing assessment of how the one true God is to be recognized. Mainstream Jews and Christians would not necessarily have found troubling the idea that God's attributes could function as semi-independent entities. Word, Wisdom, Spirit, and other such concepts had long been spoken of in such ways. It was what the Gnostics maintained about these emanations that created problems. Specifically, they maintained that the key elements Bauckham considers to have distinguished and identified Israel's God—namely, creation, formation of a chosen people brought out of Egypt, rule over the created world, and the divine name—were actually features of a lesser, imperfect emanation from the one true God, rather than identifying God Most High. Clearly this raised issues about precisely how God Most High, the one true God, is to be identified. According to the Gnostics, the very fundamental monotheistic claims recorded in the Hebrew Bible, such as "I am the LORD, and apart from me there is no other," were simply expressions of the hubris of the demiurge and an indication that he was not in fact God Most High. As we have seen throughout this book, figures aligned with and subject to God's own identity and sovereignty did not immediately raise problems. The main idea of the Gnostics, however, was that emanations of the divine essence could become increasingly imperfect, and that one (or more) of them could even be opposed to the purposes of God Most High. Here we see how Gnosticism brought issues relating to monotheism into focus. The issues raised, and the attempts to respond to them, would nevertheless prove to have implications for what until this time had been an acceptable part of Judeo-Christian monotheism, namely, the widespread ideas regarding personified divine attributes and other mediator figures.

The third century provides a suitable context for the origin or intensification of the debate with Gnosticism, and the beginnings of polemic against exalted mediator figures that had previously been widely accepted. In the second century, we see Christian theologians beginning to formulate the idea of *creatio ex nihilo*. This was done by drawing out the implications of the Judeo-Christian view of God in response to Gnosticism and contemporary philosophy, both of which held that there was an eternally existent material which God used when he created.[51] Judaism on the whole did not adopt or develop the doctrine of *creatio ex nihilo* until the Middle Ages.[52] Nonetheless, the debates about how God relates to creation may have had an impact on Judaism as well as on Christianity, even if the effect was not the same. Christians, concerned to emphasize the goodness of creation against Gnosticism, denied that God used eternally existent matter in creating, and began to define God in such a way that a clear dividing line was drawn between God and creation. This line had not previously been drawn, and the space where the line would be drawn was previously occupied by the Logos, whom Philo describes as "neither uncreated . . . nor created."[53] From the second century onward, Christians began to see the need to distinguish clearly between God and creation, which ultimately necessitated that a line be drawn on one side or the other of the Logos. And so it was, as stated earlier, that Arius and other non-Nicenes drew the line between God and the Logos, whereas the Nicenes drew the line between the Logos and the creation.[54]

The rabbis did not confront exactly the same issues as the Christians, and they thus reached different conclusions. If God's uniqueness was safeguarded sufficiently, his use of preexistent material need not be problematic. It may be hypothesized that the rabbis also participated in debates about these issues in this period, drawing a different sort of line between God and creation, one that might be bridged by metaphorical expressions of God's creative activity, such as *Memra*, but which nonetheless sought a clearer delineation than the language of previous generations provided. In response to both Gnosticism and to Christianity, the oneness of God was defined in terms of the denial of a "second power in heaven" who functions as, and could thus be confused with, God. In previous times, the distinguishing factor between the one God and other gods and angelic beings was worship, meaning specifically the sacrificial cultic worship of the Jerusalem temple.[55] Perhaps it was the final disappearance of any real hope for the rebuilding of the temple— the location where the worship that distinguished Israel's God from all other beings and powers took place—that created the need to define the uniqueness of God in more abstract, or at the very least different, terms.[56] This is of course speculation. But it certainly makes sense to relate the Jewish opposition to belief in two powers to the wider controversies that arose in this period. These debates centered on the need certain Christian theologians felt to have a clearer dividing line between God and creation, and thus a clearer definition of monotheism. The documentary evidence from rabbinic Judaism, considered in conjunction with these issues that were being debated by other groups in this period, provides a promising fit and makes it reasonable to date the origins of the two powers heresy to the end of the second century at the very earliest, and more likely the first half of the third.

What Exactly Was Heretical about "Two Powers"?

Recent scholarship has shown, and this study has confirmed, that in first-century Judaism at least, monotheism was felt to be compatible with the idea of a divine agent or viceroy who represented God and acted on his behalf.[57] This does not appear to have entirely ceased to be the case even later on. The Babylonian Talmud recounts a discussion which is said to have taken place between R. Idi (second–third century CE) and a heretic who engages in "two powers" exegesis, pointing out that Genesis 19:24 appears to refer to two "Lords."[58] It is R. Idi who responds by asserting that this refers to Metatron, who bears God's name.[59] His only point of conflict with the heretic is about whether this figure should be worshipped. The idea that there was such a principal agent of God does not appear to have been an issue in and of itself even in this later period; rather, it was *some specific aspect of the content of that belief* that was in dispute. This suggests what may have led to the "two powers" designation being applied to Christians. On the one hand,

Christians regarded the Logos/Christ/Son as "begotten" of the Father, which may have sounded rather like Gnostic talk of "emanation" to the rabbis. On the other hand, from the second century onward there was an increasing tendency to worship Christ not just in the sense that one honors God by honoring God's agent but in a fuller sense as part of the divine identity, as part of the triune Godhead.[60] The developing Christian understanding of Christ as "fully God," which was officially affirmed at the Council of Nicaea in 325 CE, led some to believe that monotheism was being denied.[61] It is interesting to note that, even in the post-Nicaea period, the Jewish-Christians who authored the Pseudo-Clementine literature did not feel that their belief in a second heavenly being, who could even be called "god," was heretical, since this figure was clearly subordinate.[62] Subordinationist Christology, whether in New Testament times or later, does not appear to have been controversial in and of itself. Within early Judaism and throughout the New Testament, no other figure is simply placed on the same level as God Most High and considered to be his equal. By drawing a clear dividing line between God and creation, the early Christians were finding a new way of defining monotheism and the uniqueness of God without needing to focus on things like sacrificial worship. But in doing so, and by then placing Christ firmly on the same side of the new dividing line as God Most High, Christians were clearly developing their understanding of God's oneness in a direction that was at the very least different from the ways of defining God's oneness that Jewish thinkers were themselves seeking to formulate in this period. Both the Judaism and Christianity of the third century CE developed and delineated their views in ways that neither had previously done.

We may thus suggest that a combination of development and retrospective condemnation were at work in the origins of the two powers controversy. It seems likely that Gnosticism, while clearly not accepted by most Jews even in the first century, was condemned as heretical when the rabbis came to have the power to do so. Belief in a principal divine agent or angelic mediator was probably not condemned until groups with Gnostic tendencies began to distinguish between the supreme God and the creator of the world, and/or until Christians began to regard the "second power" as coequal with God and equally worthy of worship. The need to polemicize against such beliefs, which developed out of earlier Jewish beliefs about mediators, but were not identical to the earlier beliefs, probably resulted in the condemnation of various streams of thought within Judaism which were felt to be too similar to the doctrines held by either Christians or Gnostics. Since they were condemned so late in the game, it may be that there was some ambiguity about which beliefs were acceptable and which were not. Perhaps many who would previously have considered themselves mainstream Jews found their beliefs being censured by the rabbinic authorities. To what extent such beliefs continued to be held in spite of official censure, and may have contributed to later mystical forms of Jewish belief, it is impossible to say. But it can be said that the developments in this period mark a further restriction of the definition of monotheism within Judaism, beyond what had been generally accepted in previous centuries. In earlier times, the decisive factor had been whom one worshipped through sacrifice. Others had wished to draw additional lines in the sand, but there was no general agreement on those matters in popular opinion within Judaism. However, in all likelihood because the Jerusalem temple was no longer there to serve the practical function of defining the uniqueness of God Most High through its sacrificial worship, it became imperative to find new ways of defining what it meant to worship, serve, and owe ultimate allegiance to only the one true God. In seeking to find new definitions, practices that had earlier been deemed perfectly acceptable came under censure as being in danger of blurring the (perhaps already somewhat blurry) remaining definitions of what set the one true God apart from all others. As can be seen from the aforementioned list of characteristics leading Christians to be grouped under the rubric of "two powers heretics," many of their "crimes" would not necessarily have been considered such in any stream of Judaism in an earlier age.

Conclusion

We have seen that Segal's work on two powers, although widely accepted and obviously a very important contribution to this field, is not without shortcomings, and at points the evidence is open to interpretations other than those argued for by Segal. It has been noted that there is no passage in the Mishnah or Tosefta which explicitly mentions "two powers" or which requires reference to that heresy in order to be understood. Alleged connections with early tannaim are also suspect in view of the late date of the documents which first associate them with the two powers heresy. A plausible setting can be given to the "heresy" and the controversies it caused in the late second and subsequent centuries, when the issue of the relationship between God and creation became an issue of debate for philosophers, Christians, and Gnostics. Therefore, there is good reason to conclude that certain conceptualities later condemned as two powers heresy would not have been controversial in the first century. In short, this study suggests that it is anachronistic to interpret Jewish and Christian documents from this period as reflecting "two powers" *heresy*.[63] Rather, they represent the form that Jewish and Judeo-Christian monotheism took in this period. That "monotheism" in early Judaism and Christianity meant something other than what it means to many today is the result of a complex historical process, wherein many new issues have regularly appeared, and new definitions have been formulated to deal with the new issues that have arisen. We do not necessarily need to think of God in the same way that previous generations did; indeed, it would be surprising if our thinking about these matters were to remain completely static for millennia. But in reading and studying these ancient texts, if we are to do justice to what they actually say, it is crucial that we respect the historical distance between ourselves and their authors, and that includes recognizing that while it is not entirely inappropriate to call their devotion to one God "monotheism," the pattern of belief being spoken about is not simply the same as the views that bear this label today, and in some respects there are highly significant differences.

Conclusion

Let us begin this final chapter by summarizing the previous chapters' arguments and conclusions. Having shown the widely divergent interpretations of the evidence regarding the relationship between early Judaism and Christianity on the idea of God, in chapter 2 we saw that Jewish devotion to one God was able to incorporate many practices that later monotheists rejected. However, this does not reflect a laxity of Jews in the Greco-Roman era about monotheism but represents a change in the definition of monotheism. There seems to have been a fervent, at times almost fanatical, adherence to the worship of only God Most High, the one true God, throughout the historical period in question. That this did not exclude the recognition of the existence of other gods, nor certain forms of interaction with them, is not a weakness of the monotheistic character of Judaism in this age. Rather, it indicates that the only form of Jewish monotheism that existed was different from what later generations of Jews and Christians called monotheism. Whether the differences and changes that resulted from later developments constitute an improvement is a value judgment that is inappropriate in the context of the historical study of this topic, since it requires the benefit of hindsight and the knowledge of developments, ideas, and issues that had not yet arisen at this point in history. While it is surely impossible to set aside our assumptions about the meaning of monotheism, it is nevertheless crucial that we seek to be *fair* to the sources and at the very least understand *why* they so often fail to live up to the standards of monotheism that many in our day seek to hold them to.

In seeking to identify the features that set Jews apart as recognizably different from other peoples and religious viewpoints in the Greco-Roman era, it was not my intention to ignore the genuine diversity of viewpoints that existed. However, the fact that non-Jewish observers recognized the Jews as having a distinctive allegiance to their God alone, and as rejecting images, suggests that these were features that most Jews held in common, or at least sufficient numbers for these things to be considered "typical." In our time we rightly seek to avoid stereotypes, and yet human cultures will by definition bear characteristic features that distinguish them from others to a greater or lesser degree. Both Jews and non-Jews appear to have felt that Jewish allegiance to one God alone represented just such a factor. It is only within the context of their perceived Jewish distinctiveness that we can make sense of the other side of the evidence. The use of amulets, the presence of dedications to the gods of the underworld on Jewish funerary inscriptions when it was possible to make or purchase ones without this element, and various other features observable from archaeological and epigraphic evidence all suggest that there was some form of distinctive exclusivity about Jewish worship that was not contradicted by these practices. In other words, these features were elements *of* Jewish monotheism in this period rather than a departure from it. In view of these latter practices, what made Jews (and later Christians) stand out in the Greco-Roman world? The distinctive core, which constituted the observable uniqueness of Judaism, centered on the fact that the Jews as a rule offered sacrifice only to their own God. The various practices discussed in chapter 2 were not felt by Jews to detract from this exclusive allegiance to one God, nor were they felt by non-Jewish observers to obliterate Jewish distinctiveness.

The differences of opinion that existed about issues other than sacrificial worship constituted elements of the legitimate diversity within early Judaism. Scholars researching other aspects of Jewish diversity in this period have noted that it was possible to agree on the authority of the Jewish Law and yet disagree on its interpretation. Some groups engaged in vitriolic rhetorical attacks on other Jews who did not agree with their understanding of the Torah. Nevertheless, these various groups, such as the Pharisees and Essenes, as well as the vast majority of Jews who belonged to no party or sect whatsoever, were all Jews, and their beliefs and practices were all forms of Judaism. The differences over exactly what allegiance to one God alone entailed, like differences of opinion about what one ought not to do on the Sabbath, were the result of differing interpretations of the sacred texts and traditions that nevertheless provided a unifying core (at least theoretically) for the Jews of this period.

How did earliest Christianity's understanding of God relate to this Jewish heritage? The axiom that God is one is stated at numerous points in the New Testament by several different authors, and never in such a way as to suggest that they felt the need to defend themselves against the charge of denying God's oneness. Monotheism was a presupposition of the earliest Christians, most of whom were Jewish themselves. In view of the importance of sacrificial worship as a defining practice for Jewish monotheism, it is instructive to look at what evidence there is regarding the early Christian practice of sacrifice. Early in the history of the Christian movement, Jesus' death comes to be understood as a sacrifice. He is never, however, anywhere depicted as the *recipient* of sacrifice. There is no evidence that the earliest Christians who continued to frequent the Jerusalem temple while it still stood asked the priests to make their offerings to both God the Father and Jesus. Such an action would have been a clear indication that the early Christian movement was rethinking its concept of God and redefining monotheism to include Jesus *within* God. But there is no evidence that any such move was made. Rather, they continued to display the same scruples regarding sacrifice as their Jewish contemporaries, refusing to offer sacrifice to the Roman gods or to the emperor. The early Christians not only remained true to the monotheistic heritage which they inherited from Judaism, but they remained *fervently* so.[1]

It is of course true that, within the course of the next few centuries, Christianity's monotheism would develop into what we today know as trinitarianism. However, over the course of the same period of time, as rabbinic Judaism came to dominance and asserted itself as Jewish orthodoxy, Jewish monotheism also developed and redefined itself. When we eventually find Jews and Christians, having developed into two essentially distinct world religions, going their separate ways over the issue of trinitarianism, *neither side* held to exactly the dynamic, flexible form of monotheism that existed in the first century. As one group was taking the heritage of early Jewish monotheism, with the room it left for ideas like the Logos, and expanding on its possibilities in relation to new issues, so also at the same time the other group was seeking to draw in the boundaries and delineate God's oneness in different terms.[2] The two definitions became intrinsically incompatible, but it has been a common mistake to assume that they always had been, that the separation over this issue had been inevitable. But rarely can anything that happens in history genuinely be called "inevitable."[3] The idea of inevitability is often simply a means for the victorious side to suggest that it was fate, providence, or the nature of things that they won rather than it being a mere accident of history. But the fact that certain developments in Jewish and Christian theology depend on historical developments that could easily have been otherwise need not be considered an argument against their importance or their validity.

What are the theological implications of this study? Some may assume that because I have insisted on the monotheistic character of early Christianity, I am in some way challenging the legitimacy of trinitarian theology. This does not follow. It is certainly true that the earliest Christians were not trinitarians in the modern sense. But neither were they monotheists in the modern sense. Perhaps the most important result of this study, and of biblical studies in general, is that the early Christians were regularly not anything at all in the modern sense but inhabited a world view and cultural context fundamentally different from ours. It is an unsettling result, to be sure, for those accustomed to read these writings as sacred Scripture, and in particular for Protestants who traditionally emphasize that anyone at all can read and interpret the Bible. The truth of the matter is that, for those readers without knowledge of ancient languages, ancient cultures, and other such subjects, the meaning of the Bible is at times not at all clear, while at other times it can seem to clearly mean things that it is unlikely to have meant in its original context. The possibility of misunderstanding for a reader today in a Western cultural setting is at least as great as the chances that the same individual will experience a cultural or linguistic misunderstanding if traveling to a foreign culture. By emphasizing these points, I do not wish to discourage interested individuals from reading the Bible in English translation—far from it. It is important, however, for all readers to understand that they are having the Bible interpreted to them by those who have translated it into their native language and are then engaging in interpretation themselves through the act of reading. The books they are reading derive from a very different world, and therefore one should not cease reading but should utilize the multitude of books and other resources that scholars have made available, expressly with the aim of helping readers make sense of these ancient texts. Having done that, one should then go on to express one's conclusions about what these writings mean with an appropriate humility and tentativeness, aware that what seems obvious to a reader today may not have been what seemed obvious to a first-century reader.

Returning to the doctrine of the Trinity, the question of whether or not the first Christians thought of God in these terms is not the only important question to ask, nor does the answer to this question determine the status of trinitarian theology in the present. That the church developed the doctrine of the Trinity shows neither simply faithfulness to nor apostasy from its heritage. It shows merely that religious traditions are living things, which by definition grow, develop, and change over time. This is inherent to the very definition of a living thing—only things which are devoid of life are completely static. In order for a religious tradition to continue to exist as a vibrant and dynamic force in each new epoch, it must *live,* and this involves constant growth and adaptation. From a theological perspective, the idea of the Trinity is an extremely helpful one in maintaining something that all monotheistic traditions have claimed to be true: that God is eternal and that God's nature is love. How can one person alone, a monad, be intrinsically loving? It is hard to imagine. The doctrine of the Trinity avoids the lonely solitude of oneness and the exclusiveness of the relationship between two, and incorporates into the very nature of God the idea of interpersonal relationships of love.[4] This was not part of the thinking of either early Judaism or earliest Christianity. However, it is a spectacularly helpful and inspiring development which may therefore be justified, if not on biblical grounds, then on its necessity for maintaining the intelligibility of certain other key concepts about the divine that *are* intrinsic to both Judaism and Christianity. And so, in short, there is not a set of obvious and unavoidable implications for dialogue between trinitarians and strict monotheists (whether Christian, Jewish, or Muslim) that results from this study. Such questions must be addressed not only biblically but also historically and theologically.[5]

Another issue that clearly intersects with the subject of this study has to do with a point of ongoing contention in dialogue between Catholics and Protestants. Was the veneration of saints a natural outgrowth from earlier Judeo-Christian beliefs? Since I did not treat this subject explicitly, the only appropriate answer I could give is to say perhaps. But at the very least, this study could be taken to suggest that this Catholic practice may not be as intrinsically incompatible with monotheism as Protestants have often accused. On the other hand, it is noteworthy that not even Jesus is addressed in prayer by the earliest generation of Christians as the saints tend to be in Catholic piety. Nor does one find in the Judaism of this period a focus on prayer to angels as mediators in the sense that their mediation is understood to be essential. Nevertheless, it is certainly possible that popular piety in ancient Judaism bore greater similarity to later Catholic piety than can be confirmed by the texts we have. But based on the evidence surveyed, the most we can say is that Catholic devotion to the saints may be as much a legitimate outgrowth of ancient Jewish and Christian monotheism as the other offshoots of this prolific parent. Like modern Jewish monotheism and Christian trinitarianism, Catholic prayer to saints bears a close connection to earlier Judeo-Christian belief without in any sense being a necessary or inevitable development from them.

New Testament theology ought to examine the New Testament depictions of God not only in relation to Christology but also on their own terms. Because of the assumption that the very foundational axiom of Jewish theology, namely, that God is one, had been called into question by the early Christians, New Testament scholars have focused more of their attention on issues of Christology. This has often led, in practice, to an almost Marcionistic tendency in New Testament scholarship—what are considered important and emphasized are the differences between early Christians and other Jewish contemporaries. However, the God of the earliest Christians was presumed by most to be the God of Israel, the God of Abraham, Isaac, and Jacob. This certainly was a universal and fundamental assumption of all the New Testament authors, and apparently of Jesus himself. Any study of the New Testament that begins from the assumption of a radical disjunction between Jews and Christians in this period on the issue of God is in all likelihood mistaken. This is not to say that there were not issues that had an effect on theology proper, such as Paul's claims about the place of Gentiles in the divine plan. This seemed to call into question many Jewish assumptions about God. However, Paul appears to have understood himself, in championing God's impartiality, as standing in the long line of prophetic critics of Israel's nationalistic limiting of God. At any rate, by showing that the early Christians did not make radical innovations regarding the *nature* of God, I hope to encourage future research to focus more on the *character* of God as depicted in the New Testament.[6] To put it differently, the question raised directly by the early Christians' innovative views and practices is not, How is God then different? but How must we think differently about the one true God if God really is at work in Jesus and his followers? The distinction may seem overly subtle, but it is still important if one is to do justice to the essential continuity between early Christianity and Judaism on the subject of God's oneness.

Another important theological issue raised by this study is how one evaluates the legitimacy of theological development. Some religious communities seek to measure faithfulness in terms of preserving beliefs and teachings as they were handed down from previous generations or as they were first created by Jesus and/or his first followers. Yet there does not appear to be any group today that could be said to hold to precisely the world view of their ancient predecessors. As we saw, both contemporary Jewish monotheism and the various forms of contemporary Christian understandings of God and Christ represent developments out of earlier beliefs, rather than mere repetitions of what earlier generations of Jews or Christians believed. This, of course, comes as no surprise to anyone even remotely familiar with either the history of Christian doctrine or the differences between ancient and modern world views. Frequently, religious communities have emphasized not the alleged *identity* of contemporary and past beliefs but the *continuity* of tradition between them. Yet even on this approach there are difficulties. For this study suggests that both Christian trinitarianism and strict Jewish monotheism are developments from a common ancestor. Both would consider themselves to have "kept the faith," while neither precisely mirrors Jewish monotheism as it existed roughly two thousand years ago. How might one adjudicate between them? Should one even attempt to do so? Or does this study simply contribute to the widespread feeling that differing interpretations are inevitable, with no real way of deciding between them? I will not attempt to provide an answer to this question in a superficial way here. Theological discussion and biblical/historical studies need to collaborate and dialogue more than they often do. However, the subject of how one evaluates theological developments is a vast one, and it would scarcely do it justice to attempt to develop an answer in the context of the conclusion of this book. Rather, having presented and interpreted the relevant historical data, the task of a strictly theological assessment must be left to others working more specifically within that domain.

Be that as it may, it is appropriate to observe that in finding a solution to this problem (as theologians must, since a religious community that cannot evaluate between differing interpretations of its Scriptures, traditions, and beliefs is hardly a healthy one), it is necessary to involve a wider set of considerations. The *process* must be evaluated, not merely the roots or the outcome. Theological developments have always been the result of the interplay of numerous factors, not simply the outworking of a linear process. Christians have always developed their theology in relation to Scripture, to worship, to experience, to reason, and to other considerations and factors. In any attempt to move forward, it will not be enough to simply return to the roots, as though one could simply return to earlier beliefs or an earlier world view and transplant it without change or modification into our time. Nor can theologians simply accept the doctrines, beliefs, and practices of their tradition un-critically, for then the possibility of a prophetic call to change seems altogether excluded, as does any genuine historical consciousness of how traditions have grown and contextualized themselves. For Chris-tian theologians, the task is to do justice to both the blossoms and its roots, to do justice to the Christian faith as it has been known and expe-rienced in recent times and to roots in the belief (as the Gospel of John puts it) that eternal life is to know the only true God, and Jesus Christ whom he has sent.

NOTES

Chapter 1

1. Larry W. Hurtado, "What Do We Mean by 'First Century Jewish Monotheism?'" *Society of Biblical Literature 1993 Seminar Papers*, ed. E. H. Lovering (Atlanta: Scholars Press, 1993), 354–55. This article is, at the time of going to press, available online at ftp://ftp.lehigh.edu/pub/listserv/ioudaios-l/Articles/lhmonoth.Z. Clearly the authors of the New Testament who affirm the Jewish axiom that "God is one" are also monotheists from this perspective. The issue then becomes how their monotheism relates to the Jewish monotheism of the same period.

2. The standpoint from which this study is undertaken represents an attempt at achieving what sociologist of religion Brian Wilson calls "sympathetic distance." I have my roots and background largely in the Christian tradition and am not unaware of the implications that a study of this sort may have for believers in churches, as well as for Jewish-Christian dialogue (on which, see Pinchas Lapide and Jürgen Moltmann, *Jewish Monotheism and Christian Trinitarian Doctrine* [Philadelphia: Fortress Press, 1981] and the contributions on this subject in Tivka Frymer-Kensky, David Novak, David Sandmel, and Michael A. Signer, eds., *Christianity in Jewish Terms* [Boulder, Colo.: Westview, 2000]). It would be dishonest to pretend that it matters little to anyone what this study might uncover. Nevertheless, I do hope to be able to "step back" sufficiently from my inherited perspectives and engage in critical reflection in order to make this work a genuine investigation rather than a piece of apologetic. If, in the process of writing, I realize that I have particular theological axes to grind, I shall try to remember to put them back in the theological tool shed until a more appropriate time. It is my hope that the reader will attempt to do the same.

3. For example, Margaret Barker, *The Great Angel: A Study of Israel's Second God* (London: SPCK, 1992); Peter Hayman, "Monotheism—A Misused Word in Jewish Studies?" *JJS* 42 (1991): 1–15.

4. See the more balanced statements by James D. G. Dunn, "Let John Be John: A Gospel for Its Time," in *The Gospel and the Gospels*, ed. Peter Stuhlmacher (Grand Rapids, Mich.: Eerdmans, 1991), 304, 315–19; and James D. G. Dunn, *The Partings of the Ways* (Philadelphia: Trinity Press International, 1991), 228–29. Dunn rightly acknowledges that boundaries were shifting in this period *on both sides* yet still at times seems to imply that it was largely the Johannine Christians who were departing from their earlier Jewish heritage.

5. Both of these viewpoints have been discussed at length in my earlier book, *John's Apologetic Christology*, Society for New Testament Studies, Monograph

Series III (Cambridge: Cambridge University Press, 2001), 6–28, and so I will make no attempt to repeat all of the arguments already made there.

6. Hurtado, "What Do We Mean," 355–56; so too Richard Bauckham, "The Throne of God and the Worship of Jesus," in *The Jewish Roots of Christological Monotheism*, ed. Carey C. Newman, James S. Davila, and Gladys S. Lewis, Supplements to the Journal for the Study of Judaism 63 (Leiden: Brill, 1999), 44. See also Adelbert Denaux, "The Monotheistic Background of New Testament Christology: Critical Reflections on Pluralist Theologies of Religions," in *The Myriad Christ: Plurality and the Quest for Unity in Contemporary Christology*, ed. T. Merrigan and J. Haers, BETL 152 (Leuven: Peeters, 2000), 144–45; Richard Bauckham, "Monotheism and Christology in the Gospel of John," in *Contours of Christology in the New Testament*, ed. Richard N. Longenecker (Grand Rapids, Mich.: Eerdmans, 2005), 153.

7. Josephus, *Jewish Antiquities* 3.91. See also Philo, *De Decalogo* 65–66.

8. Esther 3:2, 5, and particularly the additional material in the LXX (13:13–14), shows an individual who held to this scruple, but it would certainly be a stretch to move from this particular case to the conclusion that all Jews in this period would have refused to bow before any human being. Texts such as Deuteronomy 4:19 and 17:3 (see also Philo, *De Specialibus Legibus* 1:20) prohibit prostration before the heavenly host, which may provide the particular concern of some texts in avoiding prostration before *angels*, although as will be shown in the chapter on the Book of Revelation, avoidance of such homage offered to angels didn't necessarily correlate with similar scruples about human beings. In the context, however, the main reasoning is that these beings function (legitimately) as the gods of other nations, while Israel belongs to Yahweh alone. The issue of the source of the individual's authority also needs to be considered: a human being who was believed to be appointed and authorized by the one true God might have been reacted to differently than a foreigner before whom a Gentile ruler demands that people prostrate themselves. On differences of opinion regarding *proskynēsis* in the wider Greco-Roman world, see William Horbury, *Jewish Messianism and the Cult of Christ* (London: SCM, 1998), 71–75.

9. Larry W. Hurtado, *Lord Jesus Christ: Devotion to Jesus in Earliest Christianity* (Grand Rapids, Mich.: Eerdmans, 2003), 4, 31n10. On the need for a definition of worship, see also Lionel North, "Jesus and Worship, God and Sacrifice," in *Early Jewish and Christian Monotheism*, ed. Loren T. Stuckenbruck and Wendy E. S. North, Journal for the Study of the New Testament, Supplement Series 263 (New York: Continuum, 2004), 195–99; Jerome H. Neyrey, *Render to God: New Testament Understandings of the Divine* (Minneapolis: Fortress Press, 2004), 131–33.

10. See Larry Hurtado, *At the Origins of Christian Worship* (Carlisle, UK: Paternoster, 1999), 65–69.

11. Cf. P. Maurice Casey, "Monotheism, Worship and Christological Development in the Pauline Churches," in *The Jewish Roots of Christological Monotheism*, ed. Carey C. Newman, James S. Davila, and Gladys S. Lewis, Supplements to the Journal for the Study of Judaism 63 (Leiden: Brill, 1999), 217–18; North, "Jesus and Worship," 198–202. According to Martin P. Nilsson, "The High God and the Mediator," *HTR* 56 (1963): 110–11, the Jews may have been distinctive not merely because they would not offer sacrifice to other gods but also precisely because they offered sacrifices to God Most High.

12. Larry W. Hurtado, *One God, One Lord: Early Christian Devotion and Ancient Jewish Monotheism* (London: SCM Press, 1988), 99–124. Also Hurtado, *At the Origins of Christian Worship*, 91, 97.

13. Maurice Casey, *From Jewish Prophet to Gentile God* (Louisville, Ky.: Westminster John Knox, 1991).

14. See, for example, Barker, *Great Angel*; Hayman, "Monotheism"; see also Paula Fredriksen, "Gods and the One God," *Bible Review* 19, no. 1 (February 2003): 12, 49.

15. Richard Bauckham, *God Crucified: Monotheism and Christology in the New Testament* (Carlisle: Paternoster, 1998); see also Bauckham's 2002 Society of Biblical Literature conference paper, "Paul's Christology of Divine Identity," available at http://www.sbl-site2.org/Congresses/AM/2003/Richard_Bauckham .pdf/. See also the works cited in the previous note, and Karl-Heinz Ohlig, *One or Three? From the Father of Jesus to the Trinity*, Saarbrücker Theologische Forschungen 8 (Frankfurt: Peter Lang, 2002), 26–29.

16. Bauckham, *God Crucified*, 9–11. See also G. L. Prestige, *God in Patristic Thought* (London: SPCK, 1952), 98–99, on the way the divine "monarchy" or unique sovereignty was a key issue in maintaining monotheism even in the patristic period. Point 2 corresponds approximately to Wright's category of "covenantal monotheism" (Wright, *Christian Origins and the Question of God*, vol. 1, *The New Testament and the People of God* [London: SPCK, 1992], 251–52), and as the relational character of Israel's God is not disputed, nor the sort of dividing line that might distinguish monotheism from monolatry, henotheism, or the like, I shall not enter into a discussion of this category in any detail.

17. Bauckham, *God Crucified*, 15.

18. Some readers may not be familiar with the writings of Philo of Alexandria, a Jewish philosopher who lived during the first century CE. His writings and other information about him are freely available on the Internet. Those interested in further reading about his depiction of the Word or Logos and how this relates to Christology should see especially James D. G. Dunn, *Christology in the Making: An Inquiry into the Origins of the Doctrine of the Incarnation*, 2d ed. (London: SCM, 1989), 215–30; also Hurtado, *One God, One Lord*, 44–48. See also my discussion of the Gospel of John later in this book.

19. See further F. Gerald Downing, "Ontological Asymmetry in Philo and Christological Realism in Paul, Hebrews and John," *JTS* 41, no. 2 (October 1990): 423–40, on the lack of any "gap" between God and the Logos in Philo. This seems to counter Bauckham's affirmation that the Logos is firmly included within the divine identity rather than being a figure that somehow blurs and spans the gap between God and creation (*God Crucified*, 21).

20. Cf. *Mekilta Exodus* 12:3, 6; m. *Ber.* 5:5; Peder Borgen, "God's Agent in the Fourth Gospel," in *The Interpretation of John*, ed. John Ashton (Philadelphia: Fortress Press, 1986), 67–78; A. E. Harvey, "Christ as Agent," in *The Glory of Christ in the New Testament*, ed. L. D. Hurst and N. T. Wright (Oxford: Clarendon, 1987), 239–50; Hurtado, *One God*; and also Jan-A. Bühner, *Der Gesandte und sein Weg im viertem Evangelium: Die kultur- und religionsgeschichtlichen Grundlagen der johanneischen Sendungschristologie sowie ihre traditionsgeschichtliche Entwicklung* (Tübingen: J. C. B. Mohr [Paul Siebeck], 1977), passim, on the concept of agency in this period. The term "agent" used here, like the term "angel," which is applied often to Jesus/the Logos in early Christian (and

Jewish) writings, has to do with function and does not have ontological issues and considerations in view.

21. Bauckham, *God Crucified*, 27.

22. Cf. Wright, *New Testament and the People of God*, 248–59.

23. Ibid., 249.

24. See also E. P. Sanders, *Judaism: Practice and Belief 63 BCE–66 CE* (Philadelphia: Trinity Press International, 1992), 242. A striking example of the breadth of creational monotheism can be seen in Philo's exegesis of Genesis 1:26 in *De Opificio Mundi* 72–5, and *De Confusione Linguarum* 179, on which see Bauckham, *God Crucified*, 12n12.

25. Cf. Bauckham, *God Crucified*, 13–15; Hurtado, "What Do We Mean," 355–56.

26. Bauckham, *God Crucified*, 14, rightly draws attention to these passages. He fails to note, however, that they appear to be the exception rather than the rule.

27. The relevant texts are surveyed and discussed in Loren T. Stuckenbruck, *Angel Veneration and Christology*, WUNT 2:70 (Tübingen: Mohr-Siebeck, 1995).

28. Cf. Josephus, *Against Apion* 2.193, on the argument "one God, one Temple." That most Jews felt this to be the case appears to be largely undisputed. On sacrifice as the key defining boundary of Jewish monotheism, see North, "Jesus and Worship," 196–202, who distinguishes "sacrifice" from "worship," with the former being that which implies the deity of the one to whom it is offered. See too Loren T. Stuckenbruck, "'Angels' and 'God': Exploring the Limits of Early Jewish Monotheism," in *Early Jewish and Christian Monotheism*, ed. Loren T. Stuckenbruck and Wendy E. S. North, Journal for the Study of the New Testament, Supplement Series 263 (New York: Continuum, 2004), 68–69.

29. Erwin R. Goodenough, *Jewish Symbols in the Greco-Roman Period*, edited and abridged by Jacob Neusner from the original 13 vols., Mythos: The Princeton/Bollingen Series in World Mythology 37 (Princeton, N.J.: Princeton University Press, 1988), 180–88. See also Sanders, *Judaism*, 242–7.

30. Goodenough, *Jewish Symbols*, 180.

31. See my discussion of these inscriptions in the next chapter.

32. Bauckham, *God Crucified*, 5. In this he is followed by David B. Capes, in "YHWH Texts and Monothesim in Paul's Christology," in *Early Jewish and Christian Monotheism*, ed. Loren T. Stuckenbruck and Wendy E. S. North, Journal for the Study of the New Testament, Supplement Series 263 (New York: Continuum, 2004), 135.

Chapter 2

1. Brief mention of the Jewish temple at Elephantine in Egypt ought to be made at this point. The Elephantine papyri clearly give us an indication of the existence into the Persian period of Jewish cult centers that had not been subject to the Deuteronomic innovations. This is an important testimony to the relative lateness of what Bernhard Lang calls "Yahweh-aloneism" in Israel. However, one must ask whether this form of worship centered on not only Yahweh but also Anat-Yahu and other figures regarded as separate beings. If it did, how

long did it persist into the Hellenistic age? Expatriate communities, in order to continue to exist, must maintain some link with their homeland, however tenuous. If Judaism as a whole, in its expression in places like Judea and Galilee, followed the Deuteronomic teachings and sought to implement them, then ongoing friendly links with Elephantine and its worship would have been problematic. It is thus likely that either the form of cult at Elephantine changed or Judaism was much more diverse and flexible than has often been assumed. Certainly ongoing relations with Jerusalem are indicated by the Aramaic papyri.

If there is any indication as to what actually happened, it is worth noting that the petition for reconstruction speaks only of the Temple of Yahu. Does this indicate that the temple being dedicated to Yahweh alone was the norm even in Israelite polytheism? Perhaps Bethel and Anat-Yahu were simply ways of combining what were once separate figures into the identity of Yahweh. It seems that by removing animal sacrifice from the cult of this temple, the priests at Elephantine (like those at Lachish and other cult centers in the land of Israel) probably felt they were keeping in line with the spirit or aims of the Deuteronomic changes introduced into Israelite religion. To maintain Jewish identity in the Diaspora, there had to be ongoing contact with the Jewish homeland, and so it is inconceivable that Judaism in Jerusalem adopted a "Deuteronomic" perspective and those living in Egypt or even further afield escaped its influence.

A few things are certain: We cannot simply take the Pentateuch and either assume that most Jews either did or did not follow its teachings; nor can we simply divide Jews into those who did or did not accept either the Torah or the Deuteronomic perspective. As we see in the case of the Hasmoneans later on, it was perfectly possible to swear allegiance to the Law of Moses yet in practice ignore or disregard some parts of it or interpret them in such a way as to allow one's practice. Even if the Pentateuch was largely disseminated (and the existence of the Samaritan Pentateuch suggests a wide dissemination of something like the Pentateuch in its present form at a relatively early stage), the extent to which specific parts of it were known, and if known were obeyed, and the extent to which certain practices were considered compatible with its precepts also needs to be answered and cannot be assumed. But at any rate, the temple in Elephantine was destroyed in the late fifth century BCE, before the start of the Hellenistic era.

2. Many examples come to mind. The phrase "under God" was introduced into the Pledge of Allegiance roughly fifty years ago, yet my generation managed to say these words as children completely oblivious to this fact, assuming that this typically American tradition had always been spoken in its current form. Other examples include the story "'Twas the Night Before Christmas," which dates from roughly the 1820s and is today simply a traditional part of Christmas for everyone in the United States. The music to the song "Happy Birthday to You" was written in the 1890s, originally with different words, and the first evidence in print of the words that are now so familiar is in 1924, when the current words were published as a second stanza to the original ones. Few today would believe that the singing of this song on birthdays is such a recent invention. My point is that a new innovation can become an established tradition in less than the couple of centuries that passed between the exilic period and the start of the Hellenistic age.

3. Fredriksen, "Gods and the One God," 49.

4. Please note that here it is my intention to treat those who continued to seek to adhere to a Jewish religious identity. That there were "apostates" and those who abandoned their Jewish religious heritage in this period is clear, but my interest in the context of this study is in those who continued to consider themselves Jews both ethnically and religiously.

5. To avoid all contact with other forms of belief and worship was clearly impossible for those living in the Diaspora, and even for some living in Palestine. To the extent it is possible, it will be helpful to determine which acts appear to have been considered acceptable and which acts appear to have been considered unacceptable or even reprehensible.

6. Obviously the possibility of mistaken stereotypes existed then just as it does now. However, particularly in cultural contexts in which community tends to predominate over individual identity, one suspects that perceptions of major factors like religious distinctiveness, especially where there is no hint of malice or evidence of bigotry, would have borne some relation to the truth. At any rate, if we discount *both* the viewpoint of the literate elite *within* Judaism, and the viewpoint of literate outsiders writing about their observations of Judaism, then what is left is only the archaeological evidence, which on its own is ambiguous. By combining various types of evidence, I hope to do justice to all these relevant perspectives to the greatest extent possible.

7. Quoted by Diodorus in his *World History* 40.3.1–9, written c. 60 BCE.

8. Cf. Emilio Gabba, *Greek Knowledge of Jews Up to Hecataeus of Abdera: Protocol of the Fortieth Colloquy, 7 December 1980* (Berkeley, Calif.: Center for Hermeneutical Studies in Hellenistic and Modern Culture, 1981).

9. His writing is preserved in quotations, most notably by Josephus in his *Against Apion*. Since what he wrote is readily available via Josephus, I will refrain from quoting him at length in this context.

10. Lester L. Grabbe, *Judaic Religion in the Second Temple Period. Belief and Practice from the Exile to Yavneh* (London: Routledge, 2000), 218.

11. The issue in the time of Antiochus Epiphanes was not necessarily the rededication of the Jerusalem Temple to Zeus Olympus (the equally monotheistic Samaritans appear to have requested a renaming of their temple), but the inclusion of an idolatrous element coupled with the attempt to abolish traditional distinctively Jewish elements of the national religion, such as circumcision and Sabbath observance. Had it simply been a question of accepting an additional name to be referred to when discussing matters with Greek-speakers, things might have developed rather differently. In the first century in Alexandria, Philo wrote of the single God whom all peoples recognize, yet they fail to realize that this God alone is worthy of worship. His reference to this God as "father of gods and humans" in *Spec. leg.* 2:165 takes up a phrase that was widely applied to Zeus. Cf. Marcel Simon, *Le Christianisme antique et son contexte religieux: Scripta Varia*, vol. 2 (Tübingen: Mohr-Siebeck, 1981), 624–25.

12. This inclusiveness seems to be implied as well in the action of the Samaritans, who apparently asked and received permission to dedicate their Temple to Zeus Xenios in the time of Antiochus IV. See further Henk Jagersma, *A History of Israel from Alexander the Great to Bar Kochba* (Philadelphia: Fortress Press, 1986), 50–51; and William Horbury, "Jewish and Christian Monotheism in the Herodian Age," in *Early Jewish and Christian Monotheism*, ed. Loren T. Stuck-

enbruck and Wendy E. S. North, Journal for the Study of the New Testament, Supplement Series 263 (New York: Continuum, 2004), 29–30. Varro (first century BCE) respects Jewish rejection of idols and equates the Jewish God with Jupiter. Cf. Menahem Stern, *Greek and Latin Authors on Jews and Judaism*, vol.1, *From Herodotus to Plutarch* (Jerusalem: IASH, 1974), 209–10.

13. Hecataeus of Abdera mentions Jewish aniconism, which is also obviously expressed in the Jewish texts which were eventually defined as Scripture. Other key examples include Jubilees (cf., e.g., 11:17; 12:1–24; 20:7–9; 22:18, 22), Joseph and Aseneth (e.g., 8:5; 12:5–6; 13:11), and Prayer of Manasseh 10. The appropriateness of the worship of other gods by Gentiles is not seriously questioned by the Jewish sources we have, apart from in connection with a critique of idolatry, and this perhaps helps explain why there was not a strong drive to proselytize within Hellenistic Judaism.

14. See on this topic especially Tryggve N. D. Mettinger, *No Graven Image? Israelite Aniconism in Its Ancient Near Eastern Context*, CB 42 (Stockholm: Almqvist and Wiksell, 1995). On Philo's view of images in the Roman era, see Karl-Gustav Sandelin, "Philo's Ambivalence Towards Statues," *Studia Philonica Annual* 13 (2001): 122–38.

15. See Morton Smith's classic study, "The Common Theology of the Ancient Near East," *JBL* 71 (1952): 135–47, now republished in *Essential Papers on Israel and the Ancient Near East*, ed. Frederick E. Greenspahn (New York: New York University Press, 1991).

16. See most recently Hurtado, *Lord Jesus Christ*, 30–48, as well as his earlier writings on this subject.

17. For some examples, see P. Jean-Baptiste Frey, *Corpus of Jewish Inscriptions*, vol. 2 (Rome: Pontificio Istituto di Archeologia Cristiana, 1952), 373–74; John J. Collins, "Jewish Monotheism and Christian Theology," in *Aspects of Monotheism: How God Is One*, ed. Hershel Shanks and Jack Meinhardt (Washington, D.C.: Biblical Archaeology Society, 1997), 93–94.

18. P. Jean-Baptiste Frey, *Corpus of Jewish Inscriptions*, vol. 1, *Europe* (New York: KTAV, 1975), 524. The gist of inscriptions is as follows: "I invoke and call God most high, the Lord of spirits and of all flesh, upon those who traitorously murdered or poisoned wretched Heraclea/Marthina, bringing about her untimely death, unjustly shedding her innocent blood, that it might happen likewise to them that murdered or poisoned her, and to their children, O Lord, who sees all things, and O angels of God, to whom all souls this day humble themselves in supplication, in order that you [singular!] may avenge the innocent blood most quickly." Frey suggests that the day when all souls make supplication is Yom Kippur, which if correct could suggest a liturgical-cultic element to this appeal to the angels, even though in the end it is to God most high (represented by the singular second person pronoun) that the appeal is primarily made and from whom action is ultimately sought.

19. Frey, *Corpus* 1:525.

20. See also Testament of Levi 5:5; Tobit 11:14; and 11Q14. For an example of rabbinic polemic from a much later period which may indicate the persistence of this practice, see *b. Ber.* 13a. Hurtado (*Lord Jesus Christ*, 34–35) rightly suggests that the rabbis may be arguing against something that was in earlier times simply an accepted practice. For other relevant texts and their interpretation,

see Stuckenbruck, "'Angels' and 'God,'" 48–70; and Stuckenbruck *Angel Veneration*, 181–91.

21. I cannot in this context discuss the several references to Jewish "worship of angels" in the literature of the first few Christian centuries. Needless to say, most who have taken these references at face value have also regarded it as evidence of a "departure from monotheism" (e.g., Simon, *Christianisme antique*, 451–52). However, the only source I know of which explicitly uses the language of cultic sacrificial worship in this sort of context is the Pseudo-Clementine literature. In view of its references to worship of "month" and "moon" as well, the whole relevant section of the *Kerygma Petrou* can surely be considered polemical hyperbole rather than an accurate description of Jewish belief or practice. Other references may be taken to indicate reverence and other forms of acknowledgment of the importance of angels without engaging in the sacrificial worship of them. In a famous passage, Justin Martyr (*First Apology* 6.1) demonstrates a similar view from a Christian perspective. Note also Josephus's reference to the Essenes addressing the sun in a prayerful manner (*Jewish War* 2.128). On the idea of gods appointed over other territories, see also Horbury, "Jewish and Christian Monotheism," 33–40.

22. Elias J. Bickerman, *The Jews in the Greek Age* (Cambridge: Harvard University Press, 1988), 252–53.

23. Frey, *Corpus* 1:82.

24. Were we to explore this matter further here, as I will in fact do in subsequent chapters, it would become clear that the only time it is considered blasphemous to suggest another figure engages in activities or receives honors normally reserved for God alone is if the figure in question claims those attributes and honors for himself rather than receiving them from God as part of God's authorization and commissioning.

25. Frey, *Corpus* 2:444–45. See also the discussion in Martin Hengel, *Judaism and Hellenism: Studies in Their Encounter in Palestine during the Early Hellenistic Period* (London: SCM Press, 1974), 264.

26. For other instances that tested the boundaries of Jewish identity and monotheism, see Peder Borgen, "'Yes', 'No', 'How Far?': The Participation of Jews and Christians in Pagan Cults," in *Early Christianity and Hellenistic Judaism*, by Peter Borgen (Edinburgh: T&T Clark, 1996), 19–24. See, too, Horbury, *Jewish Messianism*, 74–77.

27. Borgen, "'Yes', 'No', 'How Far?'" 24–43. See further Philo, *De Ebrietate* 20; Josephus, *Jewish War* 80–92; *m. Sanhedrin* 7:6. For other instances where contact with idols was tolerated, see Horbury, "Jewish and Christian Monotheism," 35–36.

28. On attempts to eliminate elements of Jewish art that were previously accepted, see L. I. Levine, "Archaeology and the Religious Ethos of Pre-70 Palestine," in *Hillel and Jesus: Comparative Studies of Two Major Religious Leaders*, ed. James H. Charlesworth and Loren L. Johns (Minneapolis: Fortress Press, 1997), 117–20.

29. There are other key questions I wish I could answer but unfortunately cannot, except speculatively. Did the religious leaders of *early* Hellenistic Judaism consider books such as Deuteronomy authoritative? If so, how did they interpret the call to exterminate the people of the land together with their gods? Was it

simply the gods of the Canaanites and their forms of worship that were a problem? Or in other words, were all forms of polytheism equally offensive? Was the commandment to have no other god "before my face" interpreted to mean that no other God is to be *offered sacrifice* or in some other way? Could one still sing the praises of the goddess under the name of "Wisdom," as long as one did not engage in actual sacrifice to her? Was the feeling that Ba'al worship was problematic based on the fact that Ba'al was perceived in this period as a "foreign deity," representing the interests of other peoples such as the Canaanites or the Phoenicians? Within the prohibitions of books like Deuteronomy, which were gaining increasing acceptance authority, there was certainly room for more than one interpretation. And so the only indication regarding what was considered acceptable in this age is the little we know about what people actually did. On the one hand, one finds no evidence of sacrificial worship by Jews of any other deity. The case of the inscriptions in the temple of Pan is not necessarily an exception, for the reasons already mentioned. First, the inscriptions both simply offer thanks to "God." This suggests that these Jewish worshippers were identifying Pan as corresponding to their own "God most high." The possibility that some local arrangement had been made for Jewish scruples about idols is also worth considering. All other evidence suggests that sacrificial worship, which I have suggested was the key factor in how Jews understood the requirements of their exclusive devotion, was in fact reserved for the one God. On the other hand, various forms of acknowledgment of other figures were not excluded. Angels and even figures from the Greco-Roman pantheon might be invoked, or seen in dreams, without one ever feeling that one was offering to them worship or devotion that divided one's sole allegiance to the one true God. For a discussion of some of these issues, see the helpful recent study by Nathan Macdonald, *Deuteronomy and the Meaning of "Monotheism"* (Tübingen: Mohr-Siebeck, 2003), whose work suggests that in the Hebrew Bible "monotheism" was about unique *loyalty* rather than unique *existence*.

30. To return to and paraphrase the quote I offered from Fredriksen earlier, if all monotheists in the Hellenistic age were polytheists, nevertheless, some polytheists were monotheists.

31. On this aspect of ancient Judaism, see Sanders's detailed treatment in his *Judaism*, 47–118. Sanders's own treatment of the forms Jewish monotheism took in this period can be found on 242–47.

Chapter 3

1. See most recently James D. G. Dunn, "Was Jesus a Monotheist? A Contribution to the Discussion of Christian Monotheism," in *Early Jewish and Christian Monotheism*, ed. Loren T. Stuckenbruck and Wendy E. S. North, Journal for the Study of the New Testament, Supplement Series 263 (New York: Continuum, 2004), 104–19. A. E. Harvey, *Jesus and the Constraints of History: The Bampton Lectures, 1980* (London: Duckworth, 1982), with its chapter on Jesus and the constraint of monotheism, remains one of the decisive studies of this topic, although see also the criticisms raised by Hurtado, "What Do We Mean," 348–49.

2. Dunn, *Christology in the Making*, 180. See also his more recent *Theology of Paul the Apostle* (Grand Rapids, Mich.: Eerdmans, 1998), 253, where he calls it "an astonishing adaptation of the *Shema*."

3. N. T. Wright, *The Climax of the Covenant: Christ and the Law in Pauline Theology* (Edinburgh: T&T Clark, 1991), 121.

4. Wright, *Climax of the Covenant*, 129, and now more recently in his *Paul in Fresh Perspective* (Minneapolis: Fortress Press, 2005), 91–96. See also D. R. de Lacey, "'One Lord' in Pauline Christology," in *Christ the Lord: Studies in Christology Presented to Donald Guthrie*, ed. H. H. Rowdon (Leicester, UK: Inter-Varsity Press, 1982), 199–202; Donald A. Hagner, "Paul's Christology and Jewish Monotheism," in *Perspectives on Christology: Essays in Honor of Paul K. Jewett*, ed. Marguerite Shuster and Richard Muller (Grand Rapids, Mich.: Zondervan, 1991), 28–29; and Denaux, "Monotheistic Background," 150–52.

5. Philo, *Decal.* 65. See also *Conf.* 170, where he quotes Homer to make the same point.

6. Gordon Fee, *The First Epistle to the Corinthians* (Grand Rapids, Mich.: Eerdmans, 1987), 373n16 cites A. Feuillet as proposing this interpretation.

7. Some of these rulers/lords, of course, either were popularly regarded as divine or claimed divine honors for themselves.

8. See further the helpful discussion in Charles H. Giblin, "Three Monotheistic Texts in Paul," *CBQ* 37 (1975): 533–37. See too Neyrey, *Render to God*, 155, 164–67.

9. On this subject, see the helpful discussion in Frances Young, *The Theology of the Pastoral Letters* (Cambridge: Cambridge University Press, 1994), 47–55, 59–65. See also A. T. Hanson, *The Pastoral Epistles* (Grand Rapids, Mich.: Eerdmans, 1982), 38–40, who suggests on the one hand that the author borders on ditheism, while also being unoriginal in the sense that the author's Christology as expressed in the letters consists almost exclusively of quotations of creedal formulas he has inherited.

10. For examples of "lord" as a designation of figures other than the one God in Jewish literature, see Joseph and Aseneth 14:6–8, 15:12; and Testament of Abraham A 11:8.

11. Compare Philo, *De Virtutibus* 102.

12. Bauckham, "Monotheism and Christology," 164, compares such instances to the point made about Christian unity in John 17, failing to adequately distinguish between two sorts of language. One speaks of "one God, one people" and emphasizes not the *unity* of the people but that there is a single people of God just as there is only a single God. The second sort of language compares the oneness of Father and Son with the oneness of Christians with one another and brings the oneness of Christ and Christians into the mix as well. This latter language focuses on the subject of unity, whereas the former focuses on exclusive claims, and it is important to keep the two distinct.

13. Also relevant in this context is the depiction of Moses in certain Jewish writings, discussed in chapter 1.

14. So Dunn, *Christology in the Making*, 180.

15. Cf. James D. G. Dunn, *Unity and Diversity in the New Testament*, 2d ed. (London: SCM, 1990), 155–56; Ohlig, *One or Three?* 36–37. See too, however, the cautionary remarks of Jane Schaberg, *The Father, the Son and the Holy Spirit*,

SBL Dissertation Series 61 (Chico, Calif.: Scholars Press, 1982), 45–50. Although I do not have time to go into this, the reference to baptism "in the name of the Father and of the Son and of the Holy Spirit" does not reflect the full-blown trinitarian doctrine formulated centuries later but more likely mirrors the Christian creedal confession made at baptism that one believes in "One God, the Father Almighty . . . and in Jesus Christ . . . and in the Holy Spirit." For those who insist that the use of "name" in the singular proves that the three who are mentioned have a single name (which is in itself difficult, since three names are used!), I will simply draw an analogy: If a bank opens an account in the name of a child and of his parent or guardian, would any English speaker assume that there is only one name in mind?

16. Cf. Fee, *First Epistle to the Corinthians*, 373–74, and the works cited there.

17. For this exegesis, cf. Wright, *Climax of the Covenant*, 157–74.

18. Since my aim is to consider early Christian monotheism and Christology, it is important to consider Colossians, and there is no obvious advantage to creating a separate chapter for those letters whose authenticity is disputed. Hopefully the title of the chapter, specifying that this is a study of letters attributed to Paul, will enable us to set matters of authorship aside and focus on the central concern. Since the hymnic passage that is our primary interest is often thought to predate the letter itself, the question of who wrote the rest of the letter is at best irrelevant.

19. Cp. Hurtado, *Lord Jesus Christ*, 126.

20. Wright, *Climax of the Covenant*, 114, too quickly dismisses these lines of interpretation. Compare the points made by Giblin, "Three Monotheistic Texts in Paul," 535n41. On Colossians 1:15–20 in general, see especially James D. G. Dunn, *The Epistles to the Colossians and Philemon* (Grand Rapids, Mich.: Eerdmans, 1996), 83–104; Dunn, *Christology in the Making*, 187–96; Wright, *Climax of the Covenant*, 99–119; Peter T. O'Brien, *Colossians, Philemon*, Word Biblical Commentary 44 (Waco, Tex.: Word, 1982), 32–57; George B. Caird, *Paul's Letters from Prison (Ephesians, Philippians, Colossians, Philemon) in the Revised Standard Version*, New Clarendon Bible series (Oxford: Oxford University Press, 1976), 174–82; and Paul Beasley-Murray, "Colossians 1:15–20: An Early Christian Hymn Celebrating the Lordship of Christ," in *Pauline Studies: Essays Presented to F. F. Bruce on His 70th Birthday*, ed. Donald A. Hagner and Murray J. Harris (Grand Rapids, Mich.: Eerdmans, 1980), 169–82.

21. Cf. Dunn, *Partings*, 205–6; James D. G. Dunn, "How Controversial was Paul's Christology?" in *From Jesus to John*, ed. M. C. de Boer (Sheffield, UK: Sheffield Academic, 1993), 162–66; James D. G. Dunn, *The Theology of Paul the Apostle* (Grand Rapids, Mich.: Eerdmans, 1998), 252–60, 293; Oskar Skarsaune, "Is Christianity Monotheistic? Patristic Perspectives on a Jewish-Christian Debate," *Studia Patristica* 29 (1997): 355–57; Hagner, "Paul's Christology," 28–30; and Hurtado, *Lord Jesus Christ*, 165–67. Alan Segal's reading of Galatians 3:19–20 is highly problematic (*Two Powers in Heaven: Early Rabbinic Reports about Christianity and Gnosticism* [Leiden: Brill, 1977], 210–11). It does not concern mediator figures diluting monotheism. Rather, Galatians 3:19–20 concerns whether or not Moses can represent the one people of God which unites Jews and Gentiles and thus corresponds to the one God. For this exegesis, see

Wright, *Climax of the Covenant*, 159–62. The other Pauline passages cited by Segal (Philippians 2:6 and Ephesians 1:21) use language reminiscent of the later "two powers" material, but without any indication that it is controversial. I shall return to the subject of "those who say there are two powers in heaven" in a later chapter.

22. For examples of inner-Jewish polemic in early Judaism, see Luke T. Johnson, "The New Testament's Anti-Jewish Slander and the Conventions of Ancient Polemic," *JBL* 108 (1989): 436–41.

23. Frances Young notes the lack of awareness of a "Christological problem" on the part of the New Testament authors in "Christology and Creation: Towards an Hermeneutic of Patristic Christology," in *The Myriad Christ: Plurality and the Quest for Unity in Contemporary Christology*, ed. T. Merrigan and J. Haers, BETL 152 (Leuven: Peeters, 2000), 192–93; also Oskar Skarsaune, "Is Christianity Monotheistic?" 354–59; Dunn, *Partings*, 205–6. Capes, "YHWH Texts," 134, disputes this point but fails to offer any convincing reason why Paul would have so ardently defended his controversial view of the Law against objections and yet not done so in connection with his departure from historic Jewish monotheism if he had indeed made such a departure. The best explanation is that Paul did not make any affirmations that placed monotheism in jeopardy in an obvious way.

24. Cf. Hagner, "Paul's Christology," 25–26.

25. A fact to which Wright, *Climax of the Covenant*, 93–94, does insufficient justice.

26. David B. Capes, *Old Testament Yahweh Texts in Paul's Christology*, WUNT 2:47 (Tübingen: Mohr-Siebeck, 1992), 171.

27. So rightly John Ashton, *Studying John: Approaches to the Fourth Gospel* (Oxford: Clarendon, 1994), 81.

28. In later times, the Samaritans applied a similar idea to Moses. Cf. *Memar Marqah* 1.1, 3, 9; 2.12; 4.7; 5.4; 6.6. I shall need to refer to the depiction of the angel Yahoel once again in the discussion of John's Christology and monotheism.

29. Paul's use of Psalm 8:6 may indicate knowledge of the early Christian Christological tradition which combined Psalm 8:6 with Psalm 110:1. On this, see further Martin Hengel, *Studies in Early Christology* (Edinburgh: T&T Clark, 1995), 163–65.

30. See further Larry J. Kreitzer, *Jesus and God in Paul's Eschatology*, Journal for the Study of the New Testament, Supplement Series 19 (Sheffield, UK: Sheffield Academic, 1987), 116; John Ziesler, *Pauline Christianity*, rev. ed. (Oxford: Oxford University Press, 1990), 39; Ben Witherington III, *Paul's Narrative Thought World* (Louisville, Ky.: Westminster John Knox, 1994), 182–83. See also Marinus de Jonge, *God's Final Envoy* (Grand Rapids, Mich.: Eerdmans, 1998), 132–36.

31. On this point see especially Richard J. Bauckham, "The Worship of Jesus," in *The Climax of the Covenant*, by Richard J. Bauckham (Edinburgh: T&T Clarke, 1993), 118–19; Hurtado, "What Do We Mean," 348–68.

32. See my treatment of this topic in my chapter on Revelation. See also Loren T. Stuckenbruck, "Worship and Monothesim in the *Ascension of Isaiah*,"

in *The Jewish Roots of Christological Monotheism*, ed. Carey C. Newman, James S. Davila, and Gladys S. Lewis, Supplements to the Journal for the Study of Judaism 63 (Leiden: Brill, 1999), 70–89.

33. Mordechai is made to state that he would have been willing to prostrate himself to save Israel; Judith (10:23) is presented as actually doing so in order to have the opportunity to cut off Holofernes' head.

34. On the threefold classification of figures in relation to early Jewish monotheism, cf. Hurtado, *One God, One Lord*.

35. On monotheism as a pillar of first century Judaism, see Dunn, *Partings*, 19–21. On Paul's Christology as uncontroversial, see Dunn, "How Controversial Was Paul's Christology?" 162–66.

36. I am indebted here to the points emphasized by Casey, "Monotheism, Worship and Christological Development," 218–33. See further 1 Corinthians 10:14–22, which upholds Judaism's historic teaching of God as a jealous God, and the Deuteronomic depiction of worship offered to idols as actually offered to demons (Deuteronomy 32:17). See also Skarsaune, "Is Christianity Monotheistic?" 359–360.

37. For the praise offered to Jewish rulers and other relevant information, see further Horbury, *Jewish Messianism*, esp. 127–40.

38. A distinction to which Capes, "YHWH Texts," 128, does insufficient justice. The language used in reference to Jesus was certainly distinctive and perhaps provocative, but it was not for that reason necessarily any less monotheistic. See also Carl Judson Davis, *The Name and Way of the Lord: Old Testament Themes, New Testament Christology*, Journal for the Study of the New Testament, Supplement Series 129 (Sheffield, UK: Sheffield Academic, 1996), 103–40.

Chapter 4

1. McGrath, *John's Apologetic Christology*, especially pt. 2.

2. In my study I shall follow the methodology recommended by Larry Hurtado: Rather than defining monotheism in an a priori and abstract way, I intend to compare the Gospel of John to other Jewish writings whose authors would have considered themselves to be monotheists. Cf. Hurtado, "What Do We Mean," 348–68, and my discussion of this subject in chapter 1 above.

3. I shall not repeat in full the arguments I have already made in relation to this point in McGrath, *John's Apologetic Christology*, 69–147. The reader is directed to that volume if a more detailed interpretation of the most important texts in John's Gospel is desired. Although Bauckham, in his study "Monotheism and Christology," 149, suggests that John's Christology would *not* be controversial, based on their understanding of the "unique divine identity" (which was discussed in chapter 1 above), this argument would only be persuasive if one were to acknowledge that there were already precedents within Judaism to the inclusion of another figure within the divine identity (through the sharing of the divine name, for instance). Yet this is precisely what Bauckham denies elsewhere.

4. Note how language fails us in our attempt to speak in a precise way about ideas that were inherently imprecise in certain respects.

5. A number of scholars are convinced that in the first century Jews and Christians had not yet formulated a clear doctrine of *creation out of nothing*. Before the formulation of this doctrine, God was believed to have created out of "nonbeing," but that "nonbeing" was understood as formlessness, shapelessness, and chaos, the origin of which was not yet the subject of speculation and reflection. This was the view of the world and of creation prevalent in the ancient world, and there is no unambiguous evidence that Christians moved away from it prior to the second or third century. This is not to say that they were *opposed* to such a view but simply that it appears that the issues which necessitated the definition of this doctrine had not yet arisen. The Gnostic Basilides may have been the first to explicitly formulate this idea, and he is castigated for this speculation by Hippolytus. See further Gerhard May, *Creatio ex Nihilo: The Doctrine of "Creation out of Nothing" in Early Christian Thought* (Edinburgh: T&T Clark, 1994), 25; Hayman, "Monotheism," 3–4; Andrew Louth, *The Origins of the Christian Mystical Tradition: From Plato to Denys* (Oxford: Clarendon, 1981), 75–77; Young, "Christology and Creation," 193–97; and Rowan Williams, *Arius: Heresy and Tradition* (London: Darton, Longman and Todd, 1987). See also Wisdom of Solomon 11:17. Perhaps many Jews (and Christians) may have thought of God as creating *eternally*, so that there was no question that the universe's existence was ultimately dependent on God. Cf., for example, Philo, *Op.* 7, 13, 18ff. On this subject, see also Wright, *New Testament and the People of God*, 248–59; Howard Clark Kee, *The Beginnings of Christianity* (New York: T&T Clark, 2005), 448–49.

6. There was thus, in the mind of first-century Jews, what might be called a "hierarchy of being," with God on top, then his Word or Wisdom or powers, then angels and heavenly beings, and then humans, lions, slugs, mosquitoes, and whatever else, but without an absolute dividing line being drawn to distinguish God from creation.

7. For an excellent, up-to-date discussion of first-century Jewish monotheism, cf. Hurtado, "What Do We Mean?"

8. It is noteworthy that whereas in the Fourth Gospel the designation "the only true God" is addressed by Jesus to the Father and thus distinguishes between the Father and the one whom he sent, for Richard Bauckham (in his recent study "Monotheism and Christology," 160–61) Jesus is identified with Yahweh as "the only true God." Although there are helpful insights in Bauckham's notion of "divine identity," this terminology, at least *as Bauckham understands it*, appears to have difficulty doing justice to the range of statements made about Jesus by the fourth Evangelist.

9. See Hurtado, *Lord Jesus Christ*, 366–67, who notes that ideas such as Logos were not simply adopted, but *adapted*, from Greek philosophy and were used by "devout Jews (and not simply apostates or those restless with their own tradition)." Yet he follows J. Louis Martyn in considering the Johannine Christians to have been opposed for their worship of Jesus as a "second God" without explaining why Philo's similar references apparently did not provoke the same sort of controversy (*Lord Jesus Christ*, 403–4).

10. The importance of the sending motif in the Gospel of John undermines Bauckham's false antithesis in "Monotheism and Christology," 159, between agency and inclusion in the divine identity. For the author of the Gospel, the view of Jesus as the Word-made-flesh, the one who bears the divine name, and the Son whom God has sent as his agent are complementarily and not antithetically related.

11. On this subject, see further my article, "A Rebellious Son? Hugo Odeberg and the Interpretation of John 5.18," *NTS* 44 (1998): 470–73. The accusations of "blasphemy" and of Jesus "making himself (equal to) God" in John closely resemble the Synoptic tradition found in Mark 2:5–7. In Mark, some objected to Jesus claiming to do what God does, either because they felt this was something which God would not delegate to an agent or because they did not accept that Jesus is God's appointed agent. In John there is evidence of increased controversy over *the same issues that were sticking points between Christian and non-Christian Jews from the very beginning*. See also Neyrey, *Render to God*, 227.

12. Carson regards those manuscripts which state that the Father gave a name to Jesus as more reliable (Don Carson, *Gospel According to John: An Introduction and Commentary* [Leicester, UK: Inter-Varsity Press, 1991] 562), as does George Beasley-Murray, *John*, Word Biblical Commentary 36 (Dallas: Word, 1987), 293. Likewise Leon Morris accepts this as the original reading, although without explanation, in his commentary *The Gospel According to John* (Grand Rapids, Mich.: Eerdmans, 1971), 728.

13. Hurtado, *Lord Jesus Christ*, 391.

14. As for the invocation of Jesus' name in exorcism, which Hurtado mentions in this context, this is comparable to the way the names of angels are invoked in exorcisms in the Testament of Solomon.

15. See McGrath, *John's Apologetic Christology*, 135–36.

16. Both P^{66} and P^{75} read "God" rather than "Son," although they differ on whether a definite article precedes *monogenēs*. See Murray J. Harris, *Jesus as God. The New Testament Use of Theos in Reference to Jesus* (Grand Rapids, Mich.: Baker Book House, 1992) 83; Raymond E. Brown, *An Introduction to New Testament Christology* (Mahwah, N.J.: Paulist, 1994), 178–79.

17. D. A. Fennema, "John 1.18: 'God the Only Son,'" *NTS* 31 (1985): 128; Otfried Hofius, "'Der in des Vaters Schoss ist': Joh 1, 18," *ZNW* 80 (1989): 164. See also Paul R. McReynolds, "John 1:18 in Textual Variation and Translation," in *New Testament Criticism: Its Significance for Exegesis. Essays in Honour of Bruce M. Metzger*, ed. Eldon Jay Epp and Gordon D. Fee (Oxford: Clarendon Press, 1981), 115.

18. Cf. J. N. Sanders, *The Fourth Gospel in the Early Church: Its Origin and Influence on Christian Theology up to Irenaeus* (Cambridge: Cambridge University Press, 1943), 63–64.

19. The most notable instances are probably John 10:75 (reading "shepherd" rather than "door") and Luke 16:19 (giving the name of the rich man as Neve).

20. Beasley-Murray, *John*, 70. Also Carson, *Gospel According to John*, 267.

21. They may have understood Jesus to be a "second God," using this phrase in the way it was understood by Philo, Justin, and Origen. Alternatively, they may have been modalists who believed that the Son and the Father were simply

different names for the same God. That P⁶⁶ did not alter 17:3 does not tell against this proposal, since "only God" and "only *true* God" are quite different. Justin's and Origen's theology regarded the Logos as a second God subordinate to the Father.

22. Margaret Davies, *Rhetoric and Reference in the Fourth Gospel,* Journal for the Study of the New Testament, Supplement Series 69 (Sheffield, UK: Sheffield Academic, 1992), 123–24; Bart D. Ehrman, *The Orthodox Corruption of Scripture* (Oxford: Oxford University Press, 1993), 78–82.

23. For an example of a possible scribal error, see the suggestion of J. N. Sanders, *The Gospel According to St. John* (London: A. & C. Black, 1968), 85n1. That *theos* could have been added in the context of the modalist controversy makes immediate sense. The addition of *theos* to back certain theological positions is at least as likely as the accidental change to the more usual *huios,* "Son." To say, as McReynolds does, "that any *scribe* would have changed υἱός to θεός defies imagination" ("John 1:18," 114), is to show only a limitation of imagination. Carson, *Gospel According to John,* 139, is subject to a similar criticism). Cf. Ehrman, *Orthodox Corruption.*

24. Brown, *Introduction to New Testament Christology,* 179, suggests that the church fathers who quote this shorter form could be simply summarizing the verse, quoting only the necessary words. A careful examination of the patristic quotations is called for, examining each in context to determine whether this is likely to be an adequate explanation for the shorter form.

25. Cf. John 10:34, 20:28; see, however, the discussion in the rest of this chapter on the meaning of this usage. Cf. also Bruce D. Chilton, "Typologies of Memra and the Fourth Gospel," in *Targum Studies,* vol. 1, *Textual and Contextual Studies in the Pentateuchal Targums,* ed. Paul V. M. Flesher, South Florida Studies in the History of Judaism 55 (Atlanta: Scholars Press, 1992), 100.

26. I need not prolong the discussion over whether or not *huios,* "Son," originally stood in the text, since there is no real difference in meaning. Cf. Fennema, "Jesus and God According to John: An Analysis of the Fourth Gospel's Father/Son Christology" (Ph.D. diss., Duke University, 1979), 126–27.

27. Harris, *Jesus as God,* 109.

28. Cf. Philo, *Conf.* 63, 146; Philo, *De Agricultura* 51, where the Logos is described as God's "first-born" (*protogonon*). The designation *monogenēs,* used here of the incarnate Logos (vv. 14, 18), has a similar meaning. Philo also calls the Logos "eldest son."

29. The Pseudo-Clementine literature in its present form probably dates from the fourth century CE, although it very likely incorporates older sources. The similarity between this quotation and other statements of the principle of agency is truly striking.

30. See further James F. McGrath, "Johannine Christianity—*Jewish* Christianity?" *Koinonia* 8, no. 1 (1996): 5–6; McGrath, *John's Apologetic Christology,* 117–30.

31. Contra Dunn, *Partings,* 229.

32. For more on the later development that took place, see my chapter on "two powers." More detailed exegesis in support of my arguments in this chapter can be found in McGrath, *John's Apologetic Christology.*

Chapter 5

1. Hurtado, *At the Origins of Christian Worship*, 65–69.

2. As Hurtado rightly notes (ibid., 67).

3. Much attention is also given in Revelation to worship that is considered illegitimate by the author, namely, the worship of idols and/or of the beast. I shall discuss this slightly later in this chapter.

4. Now in view of the tendency in Revelation to apply the same titles to both God and Christ, it must be asked whether any of these instances of worship addressed to the Lord God Almighty or to him who sits on the throne could be addressed to both God and Christ, to both Father and Son. While not impossible, the use of the phrase "him who sits on the throne" as a designation that *distinguishes* the figure in question from "the Lamb" suggests this is not the case (cf. Rev. 4:2–4, 9–10; 5:1, 7, 13; 6:16; 7:10, 15; 19:4; 21:5). In contrast, when the Lamb is referred to on the throne, it is usually through an unusual expression such as "the Lamb (standing) in the midst of the throne" (see especially 5:6; 7:17). It thus seems accurate to say that, in Revelation, worshippers address themselves in song and prayer primarily to God and sometimes also to the Lamb.

5. It should be remembered that the most common usage of "first fruits" in the New Testament relates to Jesus himself, as the first fruits of those raised from the dead. There was a long-standing use of the term as a metaphor in Greek literature. Note also that in 14:12, obedience to God's commandments and faithfulness to Jesus are set in parallel.

6. The same issue arises in relation to the depiction of Jesus as "I am" in John's Gospel, where in spite of bearing the divine name he asserts that he does nothing of himself but only the will of him who sent him. Cf. Phil. 2:6–11, where Jesus is given the name above every name but with the ultimate aim of the glory of God the Father.

7. Bauckham, *God Crucified*, 53–54, notes the source of the title "the first and the last" in Isaiah 44:6 and 48:12. From my perspective, it can seem that such language could only mean that Jesus is identified with God in the most explicit and complete manner possible. However, the transfer of God's name to his supreme agent has already been documented as a recurring motif in Jewish literature in this period, and thus the Christian appropriation of this tradition in reference to Christ within this context would not necessarily have expressed more than the conviction that Jesus is that supreme agent. I am perhaps overemphasizing what the language applied to Jesus by the earliest Jewish Christians *need not have meant*. Even if this causes the pendulum to swing too far in the other direction, it is probably the only way to counterbalance the widespread (and historically and contextually insensitive) assumptions concerning what this language "*must* have meant." One might hope that it will eventually prove possible to attempt a balanced statement, building on the evidence presented in the preceding chapters, concerning what these authors' works would likely have been understood to mean in their first-century context. However, as I will point out in the concluding chapter, even if we reach a historically balanced and fair assessment of the early Jewish and Christian idea of God, this does not mean that we can or should revert to that viewpoint, as though we could ignore either

our own cultural and historical setting or the issues raised in the intervening centuries. At any rate, what we have here pales in comparison with the giving of the very name of God to either Christ (Phil. 2:9–11; John 8:58, 17:11) or another figure (the angel Yahoel in Apocalypse of Abraham, Enoch as the "little Yahweh" in 3 Enoch).

8. In view of 3:21, David Aune, *Revelation 1–5*, Word Biblical Commentary 52a (Dallas: Word, 1997), 352, is clearly wrong to suggest that the presentation of the Lamb *standing* in the midst of the throne relates to the Jewish reticence in later times to allow that any being could be seated in the presence of God.

9. Note also 2:26–27, where a messianic text is extended to Christians.

10. The inclusion of God's appointed representative alongside him as recipient of praise is neither unique nor without precedent (see especially 1 Chron. 29:20, 23; 1 Enoch 46:5; 48:5; 61:8; 62:2, 5–6, 9; 69:27, 29). See also Bauckham, *God Crucified*, 19–20, whose highly problematic interpretation of this and other evidence related to the current topic will be examined further below. On the custom of praying to the emperor, see Horbury, *Jewish Messianism*, 71–74.

11. Even if this were to be taken as an indication of the redactor failing to add a mention of the Lamb to an earlier Jewish recension of the apocalypse, it nonetheless remains true that the author-redactor, by not including the Lamb here, at the very least gives no indication that it was his purpose to either completely merge the figures of Christ and God or to attribute to Christ all that was appropriate for the divine within Judaism. On the significance of prayer addressed to Christ in general in the New Testament, see further Hurtado, *At the Origins of Christian Worship*, 74–81.

12. See especially 1 Chron. 29:20, 23, but also the other instances discussed throughout this book.

13. See especially 1 Enoch 46:5; 48:5; 61:8; 62:2, 5–6, 9; 69:27, 29. See also Bauckham, *God Crucified*, 19–20, whose highly problematic interpretation of this and other evidence related to the current topic will be examined further below.

14. See further Aune, *Revelation 1–5*, 355, who rightly notes that the verb *proskuneō* is "conspicuously absent" in this passage's description of the "worship" of the Lamb. On the attributes ascribed to Christ in 5:12, see Aune, *Revelation 1–5*, 364–66. The Lamb/Christ is addressed and/or mentioned alongside God in the following additional contexts: In the opening epistolary greeting beginning "Grace and peace to you" (1:4–6). There is an interesting resemblance to the Pauline equivalent, and its threefold form reflects the same Christian tradition preserved elsewhere in the New Testament. The reference to Jesus in 4:14 as "ruler of God's creation" (assuming that is the best way to translate *arche* in this context) is not to be overlooked. This is essentially a reference to Jesus as God's vice regent, the one who rules God's creation on his behalf. This resembles the status given to Adam in some Jewish literature, not to mention the status attributed to Jesus in Philippians 2:6–11. It also fits well with the other ways Jesus is portrayed in the letters to the churches, most of which open with Christological language that focuses on new creation. On the role attributed to Adam, see the discussion in Darrell L. Bock, *Blasphemy and Exal-*

tation: The Charge Against Jesus in Mark 14:53–65 (Tübingen: Mohr-Siebeck, 1998; Grand Rapids, Mich.: Baker, 2000), 115–19. The first reference to Jesus sharing his Father's throne is found in 3:21. There it is said that Jesus occupies this place because he overcame, and likewise he will grant to Christians who overcome the right to share his throne. Note also 2:26–27, where Jesus promises to share with his faithful followers the authority he has been given by God. In 14:12, obedience to God's commandments and faithfulness to Jesus are set in parallel.

15. Cf. Casey, *From Jewish Prophet to Gentile God*, 141–43.

16. On the importance of whether the figure reverenced in this way was a past worthy or a contemporary figure, see Bock, *Blasphemy and Exaltation*, 24, 29; and Hurtado, *At the Origins of Christian Worship*, 73.

17. See especially Richard Bauckham, *The Climax of Prophecy: Studies on the Book of Revelation* (Edinburgh: T&T Clark, 1993), 118–49; and Stuckenbruck, *Angel Veneration*.

18. Many of the objections raised by Jewish interlocutors in the first few Christian centuries have to do not with the things that are attributed to Jesus per se, but with the fact that they are attributed to Jesus, a man who was crucified and whom they regard as unqualified and unworthy to be regarded as the Messiah and to receive such honors.

19. Cf. Aune, *Revelation 1–5*, xcv–xcvii.

20. See the brief discussion of some of these works in Bock, *Blasphemy and Exaltation*, 118–19.

21. See the many examples conveniently provided in Maxwell J. Davidson, *Angels at Qumran: A Comparative Study of 1 Enoch 1–36, 72–108 and Sectarian Writings from Qumran*, Journal for the Study of the Pseudepigrapha Supplement 11 (Sheffield, UK: Sheffield Academic, 1992).

22. Aune, *Revelation 1–5*, 279.

23. So rightly Skarsaune, "Is Christianity Monotheistic?" 360–62. Horbury, "Jewish and Christian Monotheism," 26, interprets Justin Martyr's *Dialogue with Trypho the Jew* 8:3 as reflecting an abandonment of monotheism, but there is in fact no clear indication of this in the text. Trypho accuses Justin of forsaking the Law of God and thus of relying on human teachings instead of on those of divine origin. Even if his accusation is taken to imply that the contrast is between reliance on the specific human being Jesus rather than on God, the explicit focus on the Law still indicates that the issue is failure to obey the Law, not monotheism. The other passages he cites in his *Jewish Messianism*, 118–19, likewise do not actually question the legitimacy per se of *proskynēsis* offered to a human being. For example, 38:1 has Trypho accuse Justin of "many blasphemies," but in context the issue is not what Justin says per se, but that he makes these claims about a *crucified man*. The only place where an objection is raised that might have to do with God's unique prerogatives is in *Dial.* 65, where Trypho asks about the statement in Isaiah that God will not give his glory to another. Justin answers the objection briefly and nothing further is made of it. It seems safe to conclude that monotheism is not a significant issue of controversy in this particular Jewish-Christian dialogue.

Chapter 6

This chapter was coauthored by Dr. Jerry Truex.

1. According to Segal, the basic premise of the two powers heresy was "interpreting scripture to say that a *principal angelic or hypostatic manifestation in heaven was equivalent to God.*" See Alan Segal, *Two Powers in Heaven: Early Rabbinic Reports about Christianity and Gnosticism* (Leiden: Brill, 1977), x.

2. Cf., for example, *Mek. R. Ishmael, Bahodesh* 5; *b. Hag.,* 15a; 3 Enoch 16; *b. Sanh.,* 38b; *Deuteronomy Rabbah,* 2:33; *Ecclesiastes Rabbah* 4:8; and Segal, *Two Powers,* 118–20, 139–41, 218.

3. For early Christianity, see Mark 14:62; Phil. 2:6; Gal. 3:20; John 5:18, 6:46, 10:33; Rev. 19:11–16; and Segal, *Two Powers,* 205–19. For Philo, cf. *De Somniis* 1.227–33; *Quaestiones et Solutiones in Genesim* 2.62; *De Cherubim* 27–28; and *De Fuga et Inventione* 95, 101; Segal, *Two Powers,* 159–81.

4. For example, John Ashton, *Understanding the Fourth Gospel* (Oxford: Clarendon Press, 1991), 158; Dunn, *Partings,* 228–29; Hurtado, *One God;* Eric Osborn, *The Emergence of Christian Theology* (Cambridge: Cambridge University, 1993), 24–29; John Painter, *The Quest for the Messiah,* 2nd ed. (Nashville: Abingdon, 1993), 225; Stephen G. Wilson, *Related Strangers: Jews and Christians* (Minneapolis: Fortress Press, 1995), 79; de Jonge, *God's Final Envoy,* 141n14.

5. Segal, *Two Powers,* x, and Alan Segal, *Rebecca's Children: Judaism and Christianity in the Roman World* (Cambridge: Harvard University Press, 1986), 155, 159–60. Segal recognizes that the rabbis may not have had sufficient power in the first century to enforce orthodoxy and censure heresy (*Two Powers,* 200), but he does not appear to recognize that some would question whether rabbinic Judaism was "orthodox" or "normative" at all or only became so much later. See N. J. McEleney, "Orthodoxy in Judaism of the First Christian Century," *JSJ* 4 (1973): 19–42; N. J. McEleney, "Orthodoxy in Judaism in the First Christian Century," *JSJ* 9 (1978): 83–88; David E. Aune, "Orthodoxy in First Century Judaism: A Response to N. J. McEleney," *JSJ* 7 (1976): 1–10; Lester L. Grabbe, "Orthodoxy in First Century Judaism: What Are the Issues?" *JSJ* 8 (1977): 149–53; Philip S. Alexander, "'The Parting of the Ways' from the Perspective of Rabbinic Judaism," in *Jews and Christians,* ed. James D. G. Dunn (Tübingen: Mohr-Siebeck, 1992), 2–3, 16, 20–21; Jacob Neusner, *Judaic Law from Jesus to the Mishnah* (Atlanta: Scholars Press, 1993), chap. 1.

6. Segal writes, "It became clear that 'two powers in heaven' was a very early category of heresy, earlier than Jesus, if Philo is a trustworthy witness, and one of the basic categories by which the rabbis perceived the new phenomenon of Christianity" (*Two Powers,* ix; cf. 215).

7. For example, Segal asserts that Philo's doctrine of the Logos would "eventually [be] called heresy" (*Two Powers,* 173). On anachronism as a form of apologetic in the rabbinic literature, see Jacob Neusner, *Formative Judaism: Religious, Historical, and Literary Studies. Second Series* (Chico, Calif.: Scholars Press, 1983), 167.

8. For example, Segal muses that "even if the rabbinic evidence alone cannot demonstrate the existence of a heresy in the first century and before, it may yet

give us hints about the earlier forms of the thought which were in the process of *becoming* heretical" (*Two Powers*, 28; italics added).

9. Recent titles reveal the shift to speaking about "Judaisms." Jacob Neusner, William S. Green, and Ernest Frerichs, eds., *Judaisms and Their Messiahs at the Turn of the Christian Era* (Cambridge: Cambridge University Press, 1987); Alan F. Segal, *The Other Judaisms of Late Antiquity* (Atlanta: Scholars Press, 1987).

10. See especially Philip S. Alexander, "Rabbinic Judaism and the New Testament," *ZNW* 74 (1983): 237–46; also Dunn, *Partings*, 13. Regarding dating, see Ithamar Gruenwald, *From Apocalypticism to Gnosticism* (Frankfurt: Peter Lang, 1988), 230; Günter Stemberger, *Introduction to the Talmud and Midrash*, 2nd ed. (Edinburgh: T&T Clark, 1996), 56–59; Jacob Neusner, *The Rabbinic Traditions about the Pharisees before AD 70* (Leiden: Brill, 1971).

11. So Jacob Neusner, *Introduction to Rabbinic Literature* (New York: Doubleday, 1994), 185.

12. Cf. Dunn, *Partings*, 13.

13. "Tanna" (plural, "tannaim") is an Aramaic term frequently used to denote rabbis from the period prior to the writing of the Mishnah, the earliest work in the rabbinic corpus. Rabbis of the later period are called "amoraim."

14. For example, *t. Hullin* 2.24; cf. Jack T. Sanders, *Schismatics, Sectarians, Dissidents, Deviants* (London: SCM, 1993), 61–67. *Minim* included, but was not limited to, Jewish Christians; cf. Reuven Kimelman, "*Birkat ha-Minim* and the Lack of Evidence for an Anti-Christian Jewish Prayer in Late Antiquity," *Jewish and Christian Self-Definition*, vol. 2, ed. E. P. Sanders, A. I. Baumgarten, and Alan Mendelson (London: SCM, 1981), 228–32.

15. While not settling the issue, it is worth noting that later rabbinic writings appear to distinguish between those who believe there is "no power" in heaven (presumably atheists or Epicureans), those who believe in "many powers," and those who believe in "two powers." Cf., for example, *Sifre Deuteronomy* 329, and Segal, *Two Powers*, 8–9.

16. Justin, *Dial.* 62. Those who formulated such views may have been seeking to reconcile or harmonize Jewish beliefs with those of non-Jews or to distance the highest God from creating directly in accordance with contemporary philosophy. Cf. Philo, *Fug.* 68–70; *Conf.* 179–82; and *Op.* 72–75, and the discussions in Jarl Fossum, *The Name of God and the Angel of the Lord* (Tübingen: Mohr-Siebeck, 1985), 197–204; Birger A. Pearson, *Gnosticism, Judaism and Egyptian Christianity* (Minneapolis: Fortress Press, 1990), 34–38.

17. Cf. the texts conveniently collected in Fossum, *Name of God*, 213–20. See also Philo, *Fug.* 69, who nonetheless elsewhere emphasizes that God alone is the creator (cf., e.g., *Cher.* 77).

18. This type of exegetical argument is also found in the later targumic traditions, which draw parallels between the uniqueness of Adam and the uniqueness of God. The references to God are in the plural and explain them in terms of God speaking to the angels or to his *Memra*. See especially *Targum Neofiti* to Gen. 1:26–27; 3:22. The fact that *Targum Onqelos*, which is probably the earliest existing targum to the Pentateuch, mentions Adam's uniqueness but does not emphasize the uniqueness of God, may suggest that the plurals in the

creation stories were not the focus of intense controversy until after the interpretative traditions preserved in *Onqelos* had already taken shape.

19. See Josephus, *Against Apion* 2.193 and Wright's discussion of "covenental
monotheism" in *New Testament and the People of God*, 251–52.

20. Interestingly, Vermes reached the same conclusion about the identity on
the *minim* when looking at another strand of tradition. Cf. Geza Vermes, "The
Decalogue and the Minim," *Post-Biblical Jewish Studies* (Leiden: Brill, 1975),
176–77.

21. Cf. Neusner, *Formative Judaism*, 15–16, who suggests that the rabbis who
composed the Mishnah were concerned, if not with Gnosticism, then at least
with the same issues that concerned the Gnostics. Yet caution must be exer-
cised in view of the lack of clear evidence, as Gruenwald notes, *From Apocalypticism to Gnosticism*, 242–51. See also Nathaniel Deutsch, *The Gnostic Imagination* (Leiden: Brill, 1995), esp. 36–47.

22. Cf. Segal, *Two Powers*, 99.

23. Cf. *y. Berakot* 12d–13a; *b. Sanh.* 38b; see also *Tanhuma Kadoshim* 4.

24. Segal, *Two Powers*, 100, 152.

25. *Two Powers*, 101.

26. Gruenwald, *From Apocalypticism to Gnosticism*, 249–50.

27. The issue here could possibly be the same as that mentioned in connection with the first text I discussed, namely, that someone other than God was responsible for part of creation, thus resulting in an inferior material world. However, the specific association with Adam has little connection with such ideas.
The Gnostics did believe in a God named "man," but this was the highest God
rather than the inferior creator. The rabbinic polemic against "man" creating
would most likely have fueled Gnostic exegesis rather than countering it. Cf.
Elaine Pagels, *The Gnostic Gospels* (London: Penguin, 1979), 132; also Irenaeus,
Adv. Haer., 1.12.3 and 1.30.6. At any rate, the use of the term "partner" implies
a cooperating rather than an opposing power.

28. Like *t. Sanh.* 8:7, Philo himself asserts that God had no need of a helper
when he created (*Op.* 23, 46). Also see Hans-Friedrich Weiss, *Untersuchungen
zur Kosmologie des Hellenistischen und Palästinischen Judentums* (Berlin:
Akademie-Verlag, 1966), 320–21.

29. Segal, *Two Powers*, 49.

30. The idea of a figure other than God *sitting* in heaven is a point of controversy in later writings, and this may in fact have been objectionable to some
even at an early stage; cf. Gruenwald, *From Apocalypticism to Gnosticism*, 238;
Darrell L. Bock, "The Son of Man Seated at God's Right Hand and the Debate
over Jesus' 'Blasphemy,'" *Jesus of Nazareth: Lord and Christ*, ed. Joel B. Green
and Max Turner (Grand Rapids, Mich.: Eerdmans, 1994), 189–90. Yet what is
striking is that in the viewpoint attributed to Akiba, and in 3 Enoch, human figures are described as sitting in heaven, and it is only in later additions that such
ideas are counterbalanced in an attempt to make them seem more "orthodox."

31. So Dunn, *Partings*, 174–75. See also Wright, *New Testament and the People of God*, 259, on Jewish monotheism in this period.

32. This also appears to be a key issue in the disagreement between Justin and
Trypho in *Dial.* 38. What is blasphemous is not what Christians claim per se but
the fact that they make such claims for a *crucified man*.

33. This tradition is also relatively late, but there is nonetheless good reason for the early rabbis to have avoided mentioning it (embarrassment at the mistaken claims of a great rabbi and fear of reprisals from Rome may have been among their motives) and no real reason why it should have been invented.

34. "Blasphemy" need not imply some sort of challenge to monotheism; cf. Bock, "Son of Man," 184–86.

35. There does not seem to have been an opposition by the rabbis to messianic expectation per se in the period between the Jewish revolts. In fact, Joseph Klausner, *The Messianic Idea in Israel* (London: George Allen and Unwin, 1956), 392–96, notes that messianic and nationalistic fervor actually *increased* during this period. The problem in the case of the Christians was probably that during this period of hope for a restored nation and temple, they claimed that a man who had threatened the temple and been killed by the Romans was the Messiah.

36. Segal, *Two Powers*, 60. I presume that Segal means it was added in the latest stage of the redaction of the Babylonian Talmud, rather than being a much later interpolation. There are good form critical reasons for this conclusion, as shown by David J. Halperin, *The Merkabah in Rabbinic Literature* (New Haven, Conn.: American Oriental Society, 1980), 76, 92; see also Christopher Rowland, *The Open Heaven* (London: SPCK, 1982), 309–12. On the generally unreliable character of the *baraitot* that are found in Bavli, see Stemberger, *Introduction to the Talmud and Midrash*, 198–99.

37. P. Alexander, "3 (Hebrew Apocalypse of) Enoch," in *The Old Testament Pseudepigrapha*, vol. 1, ed. James H. Charlesworth (New York: Doubleday, 1983), 226.

38. Ibid., 226–29.

39. Ibid., 268; P. Alexander, "The Historical Setting of the Hebrew Book of Enoch," *JJS* 28 (1977): 178. See also Gruenwald, *From Apocalypticism to Gnosticism*, 229–30, who notes that the explanation given for Aher's apostasy in *b. Hag.* 15a is not the earliest one; cf. *t. Hag.* 2.3–4; *y. Hag.* 77b; *Cant. R.* 1.4; Ithamar Gruenwald, *Apocalyptic and Merkabah Mysticism* (Leiden: Brill, 1980), 90; John Bowker, *The Targums and Rabbinic Literature* (Cambridge: Cambridge University, 1969), 149. Fossum, *Name of God*, 309, accepts the Bavli account over the earlier ones found in the Tosefta and Yerushalmi for no apparent reason other than he is already convinced of the early date of the "two powers" material. Rowland's suggestion (*Open Heaven*, 334) that Yerushalmi knew the story about Aher and Metatron but chose to suppress it is highly speculative (the citation of Eccles. 5:5–6 is more likely to be the inspiration for the later traditions rather than evidence that the Metatron story was known earlier and suppressed).

40. There is some evidence which suggests that the "heresy" of Aher was Gnosticism; see Pearson, *Gnosticism*, 24; and Deutsch, *Gnostic Imagination*, 46–47, 55. See also, however, Rowland, *Open Heaven*, 337–38.

41. Gruenwald, *From Apocalypticism to Gnosticism*, 242. See also L. Ginzberg, "Elisha ben Abuyah," *Jewish Encyclopedia* 5 (1903): 138–39, who notes the unreliable character of the later Aher stories. Ginzberg suggests that Elisha was in fact a rabbi who became a Sadducee (i.e., he was an apostate from Pharisaism but not from Judaism) and only later had extreme heretical views attributed to him.

42. See George F. Moore, *Judaism in the First Centuries of the Christian Era*, vol. 1 (Cambridge: Harvard University, 1927), 365–66. On dating *Sifre Deut.*, see Stemberger, *Introduction to the Talmud and Midrash*, 272–73.

43. Segal, *Two Powers*, 17.

44. Regarding *Sifre Deut.* 379, Segal argues that the identity of the heretical group is "elusive" and that the passage could have several groups in mind. While this seems true in characterizing the passage as a whole, it is also obvious that an antagonistic form of "two powers" is particularly in view. See Segal, *Two Powers*, 85.

45. As is noted by Segal, *Two Powers*, 57. On dating *Mekhilta*, see Stemberger, *Introduction to the Talmud and Midrash*, 253–55.

46. See the relevant passages reproduced in Pearson, *Gnosticism*, 30–31; Pagels, *Gnostic Gospels*, 55–56; Segal, *Other Judaisms*, 27.

47. Segal, *Two Powers*, 262. This is not to say that Gnosticism (belief in two opposing powers) is older than other "two powers" traditions (which maintain belief in two complementary powers). Rather, it to say that resistance to Gnosticism is found in the rabbinic literature before resistance to other two power traditions emerged. The *term* "two powers," therefore, was probably first used as a reference to Gnostics and only subsequently to Christians and others with beliefs similar to theirs.

48. Cf. R. McL. Wilson, *The Gnostic Problem* (London: Mowbray, 1958), 261 and passim; and Pearson, *Gnosticism*, 34–36, 171–82, for a balanced assessment of a number of the similarities and differences between Philo and the Gnostics.

49. Cf. Neusner, *Formative Judaism*, 15–17.

50. On the question of Jewish Gnosticism, see especially Pearson, *Gnosticism*; Birger A. Pearson, "The Problem of 'Jewish Gnostic' Literature," in *Nag Hammadi, Gnosticism, and Early Christianity*, ed. Charles W. Hedrick and Robert Hodgson (Peabody, Mass.: Hendrickson, 1986), 21–35. See also Segal, *Other Judaisms*, 32–34.

51. Cf. May, *Creatio ex Nihilo*. See also Origen, *De Principiis* 2.1.4; Tertullian, *Adversus Hermogenem* 2–3.

52. So May, *Creatio ex Nihilo*, 25; Hayman, "Monotheism," 3–4.

53. Philo, *Quis Rerum Divinarum Herer Sit*, 206. See further Louth, *Origins*, 75–77.

54. See further Louth, *Origins*; Young, "Christology and Creation"; and Williams, *Arius*.

55. On worship rather than cosmology as the distinguishing feature between the Jewish world view and that of others, see especially Hurtado, "What Do We Mean," 349, 355–65. Cf. also Alexander, "Historical Setting," 179.

56. Of course, there had already been some moves in the direction of spiritualizing the notion of cultic worship, but as long as the earthly temple continued to exist, or was expected to be rebuilt, such spiritualized interpretations in no way jeopardized the boundary line sacrificial worship provided. See, for example, Valentin Nikiprowetzky, *Études philoniennes* (Paris: Cerf, 1996), 81–96, on Philo's view of the Jerusalem temple and its offerings.

57. For example, Hurtado, *One God, One Lord*, 75; Alexander, "Parting of the Ways," 19–20; Collins, "Jewish Monotheism and Christian Theology," 81–105.

58. *b. Sanh.* 38b.

59. Segal notes that it is not belief in Metatron per se that is the issue (*Two Powers*, 65). Gruenwald, *From Apocalypticism to Gnosticism*, 248, does insufficient justice to the apparent acceptability of belief in Metatron among the rabbis.

60. On the evidence of worship offered to Christ in the New Testament, see the different opinions in Hurtado, *One God, One Lord*, 99–124; Richard Bauckham, "Jesus, Worship of," in *The Anchor Bible Dictionary*, vol. 3, ed. D. N. Freedman (New York: Doubleday, 1992), 812–16; Hagner, "Paul's Christology," 26; and Dunn, *Partings*, 204–6. See also 3 Enoch 14:5–16:5, where the apostasy of Aher is almost immediately preceded by the heavenly homage offered to Metatron. On development of the worship of Christ in the second century, compare Jonathan Knight, *Disciples of the Beloved One* (Sheffield, UK: Sheffield Academic, 1996), 71–153. For an early mention, see the letter of Pliny to Trajan 10.96.7.

61. Moore (*Judaism*, 365) notes the resemblance between the arguments used in debates between rabbinic Judaism and Catholic Christianity and those found in the two powers material. The tendency for Christians to distinguish their trinitarian belief in God from Jewish monotheism can be traced back to the early third century; cf., for example, Tertullian, *Adversus Praxeam* 31.1–2.

62. The issue between the author of the Pseudo-Clementines and "the Jews" was apparently whether Jesus is the Messiah, not the idea of being a preexistent, subordinate heavenly viceroy. See further Segal, *Two Powers*, 256–58; and McGrath, "Johannine Christianity," 6–7.

63. The coauthors thank Dr. Robert Hayward for his helpful comments on an earlier draft of this chapter.

Conclusion

1. I have not entered into the debate over the meaning of the accusations that were sometimes made that the Jews of this period worshipped angels. At times this seems like hyperbolic satire of Jewish focus on calendar and festivals. Whatever one may make of these references, only two points are relevant for my purposes. First, I have already noted instances of appeal to angels and reverence for these figures which stopped short of offering sacrifice, and which thus fit within the bounds of monotheism. Second, that some Christians made these accusations against Jews suggests that, if anything, the early Christians were on the stricter end of the spectrum of early Jewish monotheism, rejecting not only sacrifice to any but God but also some forms of "worship" in a broader sense.

2. See the helpful discussion in Dunn, *Partings*, 228–29, although obviously in the coauthors' view he dates the division over monotheism too early.

3. It is interesting that very similar debates have occurred about the closest parallel in Islam to the role that Jesus has in Christianity, namely, the Quran. There have been periodic discussions regarding whether the Quran is eternal or not, which in some ways parallel the debates within Christianity regarding the Trinity and the nature of Jesus.

4. See the classic study by Jürgen Moltmann that introduced many Western readers to this idea more typical of Eastern Orthodox theology, *The Trinity and*

the Kingdom (Minneapolis: Fortress Press, 1993). See also Leonardo Boff, *Trinity and Society* (Maryknoll, N.Y.: Orbis, 1988). Other potential implications of the doctrine of the Trinity, such as for a theology of religions and religious pluralism, have also been the subject of interest in recent scholarship. For one current example, see Veli-Matti Kärkkäinen, *Trinity and Religious Pluralism* (Burlington, Vt.: Ashgate, 2004).

5. There have been a number of recent books attempting to present Jesus in a nontrinitarian fashion for a popular audience. Some are associated with Jehovah's Witnesses, while others stem from Unitarian evangelical churches. Those interested may see, for example, Anthony F. Buzzard and Charles F. Hunting, *The Doctrine of the Trinity: Christianity's Self-Inflicted Wound* (Lanham, Md.: International Scholars Publications, 1998); Mark E. Graeser, John A. Lynn, and John W. Schoenheit, *One God and One Lord: Reconsidering the Cornerstone of the Christian Faith* (Indianapolis: Christian Educational Services, 1999); Brian Holt, *Jesus—God or the Son of God? A Comparison of the Arguments* (Mt. Juliet, Tenn.: TellWay, 2002); James H. Broughton and Peter J. Southgate, *The Trinity: True or False?* (Nottingham, UK: "The Dawn" Book Supply, 2002). I mention these works here because exegetes of a trinitarian persuasion rarely interact with them directly, whereas one aim of this book is to promote a deeper understanding of the issues and a dialogue between various viewpoints that gets beyond a superficial level. These books provide an illustration of ways in which individuals committed to the authority of the same texts as trinitarians can read them in radically different ways.

6. For a helpful move in this direction, see the recent study by Neyrey, *Render to God*. Neyrey's focus is largely social-scientific, and thus more work is needed to complement this, focusing on the historical and theological aspects of this topic. See, too, the collection edited by A. Andrew Das and Frank J. Matera, *The Forgotten God: Perspectives in Biblical Theology* (Louisville, Ky.: Westminster John Knox, 2002).

BIBLIOGRAPHY

Where an entire volume of essays is relevant to the subject of this study, I have included the volume as a single entry in the bibliography. Individual chapters are cited in the notes where appropriate. I have included not only works explicitly cited in this volume but also other significant works relating to this topic to aid students and scholars who wish to investigate these matters further.

Alexander, Philip S. "Rabbinic Judaism and the New Testament." *ZNW* 74 (1983): 237–46.

———. "'The Partings of the Ways' from the Perspective of Rabbinic Judaism." In *Jews and Christians: The Partings of the Ways A. D. 70 to 135*, ed. James D. G. Dunn, 1–25. WUNT 2:66. Tübingen: J. C. B. Mohr (Paul Siebeck), 1992.

Argyle, A. W. *God in the New Testament*. Philadelphia: J. B. Lippincott, 1966.

Ashton, John. *Understanding the Fourth Gospel*. Oxford: Clarendon Press, 1991.

———. *Studying John: Approaches to the Fourth Gospel*. Oxford: Clarendon Press, 1994.

Aune, David E. *The Cultic Setting of Realized Eschatology in Early Christianity*. NovTSup 28. Leiden: E. J. Brill, 1972.

———. "Orthodoxy in First Century Judaism? A Response to N. J. McEleney." *JSJ* 7, no. 1 (1976): 1–10.

———. *Revelation 1–5*. Word Biblical Commentary 52a. Dallas: Word, 1997.

Ball, David Mark. *"I Am" in John's Gospel: Literary Function, Background and Theological Implications*. Journal for the Study of the New Testament, Supplement Series 124. Sheffield, UK: Sheffield Academic, 1996.

Barclay, John M. G. *Jews in the Mediterranean Diaspora: From Alexander to Trajan (323 BCE–117 CE)*. Edinburgh: T&T Clark, 1996.

Barker, Margaret. *The Older Testament: The Survival of Themes from the Ancient Royal Cult in Sectarian Judaism and Early Christianity*. London: SPCK, 1987.

———. *The Great Angel: A Study of Israel's Second God*. London: SPCK, 1992.

Barrett, C. K. *Essays on John*. London: SPCK, 1982.

Bartlett, John R. *Jews in the Hellenistic World: Josephus, Aristeas, the Sibylline Oracles, Eupolemus*. Cambridge Commentaries on Writings of the Jewish & Christian World 200 BC to AD 200, vol. 1, pt. 1. Cambridge: Cambridge University Press, 1985.

Bauckham, Richard. "Jesus, Worship of." In *The Anchor Bible Dictionary*, vol. 3, ed. David N. Freedman, 812–19. Garden City, N.Y.: Doubleday, 1992.

Bauckham, Richard J. "The Worship of Jesus." In *The Climax of Prophecy: Studies on the Book of Revelation*, by Richard J. Bauckham, 118–49. Edinburgh: T&T Clark, 1993. Reprinted, with minor revisions, from "The Worship of Jesus in Early Christianity." *NTS* 27 (1980–81): 322–41.

———. "The Worship of Jesus." In *The Anchor Bible Dictionary*, vol. 3, ed. David Noel Freedman, 812–19. Garden City, N.Y.: Doubleday, 1992.

———. *God Crucified: Monotheism and Christology in the New Testament*. Carlisle, UK: Paternoster, 1998.

———. "Monotheism and Christology in the Gospel of John." In *Contours of Christology in the New Testament*, ed. Richard N. Longenecker, 148–66. Grand Rapids, Mich.: Eerdmans, 2005.

Beasley-Murray, George R. *Revelation*. New Century Bible Commentary. Grand Rapids, Mich.: Eerdmans; London: Marshall, Morgan & Scott, 1974.

———. *John*. Word Biblical Commentary 36. Dallas: Word, 1987.

Beasley-Murray, Paul. "Colossians 1:15–20: An Early Christian Hymn Celebrating the Lordship of Christ." In *Pauline Studies: Essays Presented to F. F. Bruce on His 70th Birthday*, ed. D. A. Hagner and M. J. Harris, 169–83. Exeter, UK: Paternoster, 1980.

Berger, Peter, and Thomas Luckmann. *The Social Construction of Reality: A Treatise in the Sociology of Knowledge*. London: Allen Lane/Penguin Press, 1967.

Bock, Darrell L. "The Son of Man Seated at God's Right Hand and the Debate over Jesus' 'Blasphemy.'" In *Jesus of Nazareth: Lord and Christ: Essays on the Historical Jesus and New Testament Christology*, ed. Joel B. Green and Max Turner, 181–91. Grand Rapids, Mich.: Eerdmans, 1994.

Bockmuehl, Markus. *This Jesus: Martyr, Lord, Messiah*. Edinburgh: T&T Clark, 1994.

Borgen, Peder. "God's Agent in the Fourth Gospel." In *The Interpretation of John*, ed. John Ashton, 67–78. Issues in Religion and Theology 9. Philadelphia: Fortress Press; London: SPCK, 1986.

———. "Creation, Logos and the Son: Observations on John 1:1–18 and 5:17–18." *Ex Auditu* 3 (1987): 88–97.

———. *Philo, John and Paul: New Perspectives on Judaism and Early Christianity*. Brown Judaic Studies 131. Atlanta: Scholars Press, 1987.

———. *Early Christianity and Hellenistic Judaism*. Edinburgh: T&T Clark, 1996.

———. "The Gospel of John and Hellenism. Some Observations." In *Exploring the Gospel of John: In Honor of D. Moody Smith*, ed. R. Alan Culpepper and C. Clifton Black, 98–123. Louisville, Ky.: Westminster John Knox Press, 1996.

Bowman, John. *The Samaritan Problem: Studies in the Relationships of Samaritanism, Judaism, and Early Christianity*. Pittsburgh Theological Monograph Series 4. Pittsburgh: Pickwick Press, 1975.

Brown, Colin. "Trinity and Incarnation: In Search of Contemporary Orthodoxy." *Ex Auditu* 7 (1991): 83–100.

Brown, Raymond E. *An Introduction to New Testament Christology*. Mahway, N.J.: Paulist Press, 1994.

Bruce, F. F. *The Book of the Acts*. Rev. ed. New International Commentary on the New Testament. Grand Rapids, Mich.: Eerdmans, 1988.

———. *The Epistle to the Hebrews*. Rev. ed. New International Commentary on the New Testament. Grand Rapids, Mich.: Eerdmans, 1990.

Buchanan, George Wesley. "The Samaritan Origin of the Gospel of John." In *Religions in Antiquity: Essays in Memory of Erwin Ramsell Goodenough*, ed. Jacob Neusner, 149–75. Leiden: E. J. Brill, 1968.

———. "Apostolic Christology." In *Society of Biblical Literature Seminar Papers, 1986*, ed. K. H. Richards, 172–82. Atlanta: Scholars Press, 1986.

Bühner, J.-A. *Der Gesandte und sein Weg im viertem Evangelium: Die kulturund religionsgeschichtlichen Grundlagen der johanneischen Sendungschristologie sowie ihre traditionsgeschichtliche Entwicklung*. Tübingen: J. C. B. Mohr (Paul Siebeck), 1977.

Burge, Gary M. "'I Am' Sayings." In *Dictionary of Jesus and the Gospels*, ed. Joel B. Green, Scot McKnight, and I. Howard Marshall, 354–56. Leicester, UK: Inter-Varsity Press, 1992.

Caird, George B. *Paul's Letters from Prison (Ephesians, Philippians, Colossians, Philemon) in the Revised Standard Version*. New Clarendon Bible series. Oxford: Oxford University Press, 1976.

Callan, Terrance. "The Exegetical Background of Gal. 3:19b." *JBL* 99 (1980): 549–67.

Capes, David B. *Old Testament Yahweh Texts in Paul's Christology*. WUNT 2:47. Tübingen: J. C. B. Mohr (Paul Siebeck), 1992.

Carrell, Peter R. *Jesus and the Angels: Angelology and the Christology of the Apocalypse of John*. Society for New Testament Studies, Monograph Series 95. Cambridge: Cambridge University Press, 1997.

Carson, Don A. *The Gospel According to John: An Introduction and Commentary*. Grand Rapids, Mich.: Eerdmans, 1991.

Casey, Maurice. *From Jewish Prophet to Gentile God: The Origins and Development of New Testament Christology*. The Edward Cadbury Lectures at the University of Birmingham, 1985–86. Cambridge: James Clarke, 1991.

———. *Is John's Gospel True?* London: Routledge, 1996.

Chester, Andrew. "Jewish Messianic Expectations and Mediatorial Figures and Pauline Christology." In *Paulus und das antike Judentum*, ed. Martin Hengel and Ulrich Heckel, 17–89. WUNT 2:58. Tübingen: J. C. B. Mohr (Paul Siebeck), 1991.

Chilton, Bruce D. "Typologies of Memra and the Fourth Gospel." In *Targum Studies*. Vol. 1, *Textual and Contextual Studies in the Pentateuchal Targums*, ed. Paul V. M. Flesher, 89–100. South Florida Studies in the History of Judaism 55. Atlanta: Scholars Press, 1992.

Cohon, Samuel S. "The Unity of God. A Study in Hellenistic and Rabbinic Theology." *HUCA* 26 (1955): 425–79.

Collins, John J. "The Son of Man in First-Century Judaism." *NTS* 38 (1992): 448–66.

———. "A Throne in the Heavens." In *The Scepter and the Star: The Messiahs of the Dead Sea Scrolls and Other Ancient Literature*. New York: Doubleday, 1995.

———. "Jewish Monotheism and Christian Theology." In *Aspects of Monotheism: How God Is One*, ed. Hershel Shanks and Jack Meinhardt, 81–105. Symposium at the Smithsonian Institution, October 19, 1996. Washington, D.C.: Biblical Archaeology Society, 1997.

Coppens, J., ed. *La Notion biblique de Dieu: Le Dieu de la Bible et le Dieu des philosophes*. BETL 41. Leuven, Belgium: Leuven University Press, 1976.

Crump, David. *Jesus the Intercessor: Prayer and Christology in Luke–Acts*. Grand Rapids, Mich.: Baker, 1999.

Culianu, Ioan P. "The Angels of the Nations and the Origins of Gnostic Dualism." In *Studies in Gnosticism and Hellenistic Religions: Festschrift for G. Quispel*, ed. R. van den Broek and M. J. Vermaseren, 78–91. Études préliminaires aux religions orientales dans l'Empire Romain 91. Leiden: Brill, 1981.

Dahl, Nils A. "The One God of Jews and Gentiles (Romans 3:29–30)." In *Studies in Paul: Theology for the Early Christian Mission*, by Nils A. Dahl, 178–91. Minneapolis: Fortress Press, 1977.

Daniélou, Jean. *A History of Early Christian Doctrine before the Council of Nicaea*. Vol. 1, *The Theology of Jewish Christianity*. London: Darton, Longman and Todd, 1964.

Davies, J. G. *He Ascended into Heaven: A Study in the History of Doctrine*. Bampton Lectures 1958. London: Lutterworth Press, 1958.

Davies, Margaret. *Rhetoric and Reference in the Fourth Gospel*. Journal for the Study of the New Testament, Supplement Series 69. Sheffield, UK: Sheffield Academic, 1992.

Davies, W. D. *Paul and Rabbinic Judaism: Some Rabbinic Elements in Pauline Theology*. 2nd ed. London: SPCK, 1955.

Davis, P. G. "Divine Agents, Mediators, and New Testament Christology." *JTS* 45 (1994): 478–503.

Davis, Stephen T., Daniel Kendall, and Gerald O'Collins, eds. *The Trinity: An Interdisciplinary Symposium on the Trinity*. Oxford: Oxford University Press, 1999.

Dean-Otting, Mary. *Heavenly Journeys: A Study of the Motif in Hellenistic Jewish Literature*. Judentum und Umwelt 8. Frankfurt: Verlag Peter Lang, 1984.

Di Segni, Leah. "Εἰς Θεος in Palestinian Inscriptions." *SCI* 13 (1994): 94–115.

Dietrich, Walter, and Martin Klopfenstein, eds. *Ein Got allein?* Freiburg: Universitätsverlag Freiburg (Schweiz); Göttingen: Vandenhoeck & Ruprecht, 1994.

Dodd, C. H. *The Interpretation of the Fourth Gospel*. Cambridge: Cambridge University Press, 1953.

———. *Historical Tradition in the Fourth Gospel*. Cambridge: Cambridge University Press, 1963.

———. "A Hidden Parable in the Fourth Gospel." In *More New Testament Studies*, by C. H. Dodd, 30–40. Manchester: Manchester University Press, 1968.

Donahue, John R. "A Neglected Factory in the Theology of Mark." *JBL* 101 (1982): 563–94.

Downing, F. Gerald. "Ontological Asymmetry in Philo and Christological Realism in Paul, Hebrews and John." *JTS* 41, no. 2 (October 1990): 423–40.

Dunn, James D. G. "Was Christianity a Monotheistic Faith from the Beginning?" *SJT* 35 (1982): 303–36.

———. "Some Clarifications on Issues of Method: A Reply to Holliday and Segal." *Semeia* 30 (1984): 97–104.

———. *Romans 1–8*. Word Biblical Commentary 38A. Dallas: Word, 1988.

———. *Romans 9–16*. Word Biblical Commentary 38B. Dallas: Word, 1988.

———. *Christology in the Making: An Inquiry into the Origins of the Doctrine of the Incarnation.* 2nd ed. London: SCM Press, 1989.

———. *Jesus, Paul and the Law. Studies in Mark and Galatians.* London: SPCK, 1990.

———. *Unity and Diversity in the New Testament: An Inquiry into the Character of Earliest Christianity.* 2nd ed. London: SCM Press, 1990.

———. "John and the Oral Gospel Tradition." In *Jesus and the Oral Gospel Tradition,* ed. Henry Wansbrough, 351–79. Journal for the Study of the New Testament, Supplement Series 64. Sheffield, UK: Sheffield Academic, 1991.

———. "Let John Be John: A Gospel for Its Time." In *The Gospel and the Gospels,* ed. Peter Stuhlmacher, 293–322. Grand Rapids, Mich.: Eerdmans, 1991.

———. *The Partings of the Ways Between Judaism and Christianity and Their Significance for the Character of Christianity.* London: SCM Press, 1991.

———. "Christology (NT)." In *The Anchor Bible Dictionary.* Vol. 1, *A–C,* ed. David N. Freedman, 978–91. New York: Doubleday, 1992.

———. "Incarnation." In *The Anchor Bible Dictionary.* Vol. 3, *H–J,* ed. David N. Freedman, 397–404. New York: Doubleday, 1992.

———. "Christology as an Aspect of Theology." In *The Future of Christology: Essays in Honor of Leander E. Keck.,* ed. Abraham J. Malherbe and Wayne A. Meeks, 202–12. Minneapolis: Fortress Press, 1993.

———. "The Making of Christology—Evolution or Unfolding?" In *Jesus of Nazareth, Lord and Christ: Essays on the Historical Jesus and New Testament Christology,* ed. Joel B. Green and Max Turner, 437–52. Grand Rapids, Mich.: Eerdmans, 1994.

———. "The Colossian Philosophy: A Confident Jewish Apologia." *Biblica* 76 (1995): 153–81.

———. *The Epistles to the Colossians and to Philemon: A Commentary on the Greek Text.* New International Greek Testament Commentary. Grand Rapids, Mich.: Eerdmans; Carlisle, UK: Paternoster, 1996.

———. *The Theology of Paul the Apostle.* Grand Rapids, Mich.: Eerdmans; Edinburgh: T&T Clark, 1998.

Ehrman, Bart D. *The Orthodox Corruption of Scripture: The Effect of Early Christological Controversy on the Text of the New Testament.* Oxford: Oxford University Press, 1993.

Ellis, E. Earle. "Deity-Christology in Mark 14:58." In *Jesus of Nazareth, Lord and Christ: Essays on the Historical Jesus and New Testament Christology,* ed. Joel B. Green and Max Turner, 192–203. Grand Rapids, Mich.: Eerdmans, 1994.

Eltester, Walther. "Der Logos und Sein Prophet. Fragen zur heutigen Erklärung des johanneischen Prologs." In *Apophoreta: Festschrift für Ernst Haenchen,* ed. Walther Eltester, 109–34. BZNW 30. Berlin: Alfred Töpelmann, 1964.

Epp, Eldon Jay. "Wisdom, Torah, Word: The Johannine Prologue and the Purpose of the Fourth Gospel." In *Current Issues in Biblical and Patristic Interpretation: Studies in Honor of Merrill C. Tenney Presented by his Former Students,* ed. Gerald F. Hawthorne, 128–46. Grand Rapids, Mich.: Eerdmans, 1975.

Evans, Craig A. *Word and Glory: On the Exegetical and Theological Background of John's Prologue.* Journal for the Study of the New Testament, Supplement Series 89. Sheffield, UK: Sheffield Academic, 1993.

———. *Jesus and His Contemporaries: Comparative Studies.* AGAJU 25. Leiden: E. J. Brill, 1995.

Fennema, D. A. "Jesus and God According to John: An Analysis of the Fourth Gospel's Father/Son Christology." Ph.D. diss., Duke University, 1979.

———. "John 1.18: 'God the Only Son.'" *NTS* 31 (1985): 124–35.

Fletcher-Louis, Crispin H. T. *Luke–Acts: Angels, Christology and Soteriology.* WUNT 2:94. Tübingen: Mohr-Siebeck, 1997.

Fossum, Jarl E. *The Name of God and the Angel of the Lord: Samaritan and Jewish Concepts of Intermediation and the Origin of Gnosticism.* WUNT 2:36. Tübingen: J. C. B. Mohr (Paul Siebeck), 1985.

———. "Colossians 1.15–18a in the Light of Jewish Mysticism and Gnosticism." *NTS* 35 (1989): 183–201.

———. "The *New Religionsgeschichtliche Schule*: The Quest for Jewish Christology." In *Society of Biblical Literature 1991 Seminar Papers*, ed. Eugene H. Lovering, 638–46. Atlanta: Scholars Press, 1991.

———. *The Image of the Invisible God: Essays on the Influence of Jewish Mysticism on Early Christology.* Novum Testamentum et orbis antiquus 30. Freiburg: Universitätsverlag Freiburg (Schweiz); Göttingen: Vandenhoeck & Ruprecht, 1995.

Fowden, Garth. *Empire to Commonwealth: Consequences of Monotheism in Late Antiquity.* Princeton, N.J.: Princeton University Press, 1993.

Fowler, William Warde. *Roman Ideas of Deity in the Last Century Before the Christian Era: Lectures Delivered in Oxford for the Common University Fund.* Freeport, N.Y.: Books for Libraries Press, 1969.

France, R. T. "The Worship of Jesus: A Neglected Factor in Christological Debate?" In *Christ the Lord: Studies in Christology Presented to Donald Guthrie*, ed. Harold H. Rowdon, 17–36. Leicester, UK: Inter-Varsity Press, 1982.

———. "Development in New Testament Christology." In *Crisis in Christology. Essays in Quest of Resolution*, ed. William R. Farmer, 63–82. Livonia, Minn.: Dove Booksellers, 1995.

Fuller, Reginald H. *The Foundations of New Testament Christology.* New York: Scribners, 1965.

———. "The Incarnation in Historical Perspective." In *Theology and Culture. Essays in Honor of A. T. Mollegen and C. L. Stanley*, ed. W. Taylor Stevenson, 57–66. *Anglican Theological Review*, Supplementary Series 7 (November 1976).

———. "Lower and Higher Christology in the Fourth Gospel." In *The Conversation Continues: Studies in Paul and John in Honor of J. Louis Martyn*, ed. R. T. Fortna and B. R. Gaventa, 357–65. Nashville: Abingdon Press, 1990.

Gager, John G. *The Origins of Anti-Semitism: Attitudes Toward Judaism in Pagan and Christian Antiquity.* Oxford: Oxford University Press, 1983.

Gerhardson, Birger. "Monoteism och högkristologi I Matteusevangeliet." *SEA* 37–38 (1972–73): 125–44.

Gese, Hartmut. "Wisdom, Son of Man, and the Origins of Christology: The Consistent Development of Biblical Theology." *HBT* 3 (1981): 23–57.

Gieschen, Charles A. *Angelomorphic Christology: Antecedents and Early Evidence.* AGAJU 42. Leiden: Brill, 1998.

Ginzberg, L. "Elisha ben Abuyah." *Jewish Encyclopaedia* 5 (1903): 138–39.

Goldstein, Jonathan A. "Jewish Acceptance and Rejection of Hellenism." In *Jewish and Christian Self-Definition.* Vol. 2, *Aspects of Judaism in the Greco-Roman Period,* ed. E. P. Sanders, A. I. Baumgarten, and Alan Mendelson, 64–87. London: SCM Press, 1981.

Goodenough, Erwin R. *Jewish Symbols in the Greco-Roman Period.* Edited and abridged by Jacob Neusner from the original 13 vols. Mythos: The Princeton/Bollingen Series in World Mythology 37. Princeton, N.J.: Princeton University Press, 1988.

Grabbe, Lester L. "Orthodoxy in First Century Judaism: What Are the Issues?" *JSJ* 8, no. 2 (1977): 149–53.

Grant, Robert M. *Gods and the One God.* Philadelphia: Westminster, 1986.

Grässer, Erich. "'God Is One' (Rom. 3:30)." In *"Ich will euer Gott werden": Beispiele biblischenRedens von Gott,* by Erich Grässer, 179–205. Stuttgarter Bibelstudien 100. Stuttgart: Katholisches Bibelwerk, 1981.

Green, Joel B., and Max Turner, eds. *Jesus of Nazareth, Lord and Christ: Essays on the Historical Jesus and New Testament Christology.* Carlisle, UK: Paternoster; Grand Rapids, Mich.: Eerdmans, 1994.

Gruenwald, Ithamar. *From Apocalypticism to Gnosticism.* Beiträge zur Erforschung des Alten Testaments und des antiken Judentums 14. Frankfurt: Peter Lang, 1988.

Habermann, Jürgen. *Präexistenzaussagen im Neuen Testament.* EHS 23:362. Frankfurt: Peter Lang, 1990.

Hagner, Donald A. "Paul's Christology and Jewish Monotheism." In *Perspectives on Christology: Essays in Honor of Paul K. Jewett,* ed. Marguerite Shuster and Richard A. Muller, 19–38. Grand Rapids, Mich.: Zondervan, 1991.

Hahn, Ferdinand. "The Confession of the One God in the New Testament." *HTR* 2 (1980): 69–84.

Halperin, David J. *The Merkabah in Rabbinic Literature.* American Oriental Series 62. New Haven, Conn.: American Oriental Society, 1980.

Hamerton-Kelly, R. G. *Pre-existence, Wisdom, and the Son of Man: A Study in the Idea of Pre-existence in the New Testament.* Society for New Testament Studies, Monograph Series 21. Cambridge: Cambridge University Press, 1973.

Hannah, Darrell D. *Michael and Christ: Michael Traditions and Angel Christology in Early Christianity.* WUNT 2:109. Tübingen: Mohr-Siebeck, 1999.

Hanson, Anthony Tyrell. *Jesus Christ in the Old Testament.* London: SPCK, 1965.

Hanson, R. P. C. *The Search for the Christian Doctrine of God: The Arian Controversy, 318–381.* Edinburgh: T&T Clark, 1988.

Harner, Philip B. *The "I Am" of the Fourth Gospel.* Facet Books, Biblical Series 26. Philadelphia: Fortress Press, 1970.

Harrelson, Walter, and Randall M. Falk. *Jews and Christians: A Troubled Family.* Nashville: Abingdon, 1990.

Harris, Murray J. *Jesus as God: The New Testament Use of Theos in Reference to Jesus.* Grand Rapids, Mich.: Baker Book House, 1992.

Harshbarger, Luther H., and John A. Mourant. *Judaism and Christianity: Perspectives and Traditions.* Boston: Allyn and Bacon, 1968.

Hartill, Percy. *The Unity of God: A Study in Christian Monotheism.* London: A. R. Mowbray; New York: Morehouse-Gorham, 1952.

Hartin, P. J. "A Community in Crisis: The Christology of the Johannine Community as the Point at Issue." *Neotestamentica* 19 (1985): 37–49.

Hartman, Lars. "Johannine Jesus-Belief and Monotheism." In *Aspects of the Johannine Literature,* ed. L. Hartman and B. Olsson, 85–99. Coniectanea Biblica, NT Series 18. Uppsala: Almqvist and Wiksell, 1987.

Harvey, A. E. *Jesus and the Constraints of History: The Bampton Lectures, 1980.* London: Duckworth, 1982.

———. "Christ as Agent." In *The Glory of Christ in the New Testament,* ed. L. D. Hurst and N. T. Wright, 239–50. Oxford: Clarendon Press, 1987.

Harvey, Graham. *The True Israel: Uses of the Names Jew, Hebrew and Israel in Ancient Jewish and Early Christian Literature.* AGAJU 35. Leiden: E. J. Brill, 1996.

Hay, David M. *Glory at the Right Hand: Psalm 110 in Early Christianity.* Nashville: Abingdon Press, 1973.

Hayman, Peter. "Monotheism—A Misused Word in Jewish Studies?" *JJS* 42 (1991): 1–15.

Hayward, C. T. R. "The Holy Name of the God of Moses and the Prologue of St. John's Gospel." *NTS* 25 (1978): 16–32.

Hellwig, Monika K. "From Christ to God: The Christian Perspective." In *Jews and Christians Speak of Jesus,* ed. Arthur E. Zannoni, 137–49. Minneapolis: Fortress Press, 1994.

Hengel, Martin. *Judaism and Hellenism: Studies in Their Encounter in Palestine during the Early Hellenistic Period.* London: SCM Press, 1974.

———. *Between Jesus and Paul: Studies in the Earliest History of Christianity.* London: SCM Press, 1983.

———. *The "Hellenization" of Judaea in the First Century after Christ.* London: SCM Press, 1989.

———. *Studies in Early Christology.* Edinburgh: T&T Clark, 1995.

Hofius, Otfried. "'Der in des Vaters Schoss ist': Joh 1, 18." *ZNW* 80 (1989): 163–71.

Hofrichter, Peter. "Logoslehre und Gottesbild bei Apologeten, Modalisten und Gnostikern: Johanneische Christologie im Lichte ihrer frühesten Rezeption." In *Monotheismus und Christologie. Zur Gottesfrage im Hellenistischen Judentum und im Urchristentum,* ed. Hans-Josef Klauck, 186–217. Quaestiones Disputatae 138. Freiburg: Herder, 1992.

Holtz, Traugott. "Gott in der Apokalypse." In *L'Apocalypse johannique et l'Apocalyptique dans le Nouveau Testament,* ed. J. Lambrecht, 247–65. BETL 53. Leuven: Leuven University Press, 1980.

———. "Theo-logie und Christologie bei Paulus." In *Glaube und Eschatologie: Festschrift für Werner Georg Kümmel zum 80 Geburtstag,* ed. E. Grässer and O. Merk, 105–21. Tübingen: J. C. B. Mohr (Paul Siebeck), 1985.

Hooker, Morna D. "Were There False Teachers in Colossae?" In *Christ and Spirit in the New Testament: Studies in Honour of C. F. D. Moule,* ed. Barnabas Lindars and Stephen S. Smalley, 315–31. Cambridge: Cambridge University Press, 1973.

————. *From Adam to Christ: Essays on Paul.* Cambridge: Cambridge University Press, 1990.

Horbury, William. *Jewish Messianism and the Cult of Christ.* London: SCM, 1998.

Howard, George. "Phil 2:6–11 and the Human Christ." *CBQ* 40 (1978): 368–87.

Hurst, L. D. "The Christology of Hebrews 1 and 2." In *The Glory of Christ in the New Testament: Studies in Christology in Memory of G. B. Caird,* ed. L. D. Hurst and N. T. Wright, 151–64. Oxford: Clarendon Press, 1987.

Hurtado Larry W. *One God, One Lord: Early Christian Devotion and Ancient Jewish Monotheism.* London: SCM Press, 1988.

————. "What Do We Mean by 'First-Century Jewish Monotheism'?" In *Society of Biblical Literature 1993 Seminar Papers,* ed. Eugene M. Lovering Jr., 348–68. Atlanta: Scholars Press, 1993.

————. "Christ-Devotion in the First Two Centuries: Reflections and a Proposal." *Toronto Journal of Theology* 12, no. 1 (1996): 17–33.

————. "First-Century Jewish Monotheism." *Journal for the Study of the New Testament* 71 (1998): 3–26.

————. *At the Origins of Christian Worship.* Carlisle, UK: Paternoster, 1999.

————. *Lord Jesus Christ: Devotion to Jesus in Earliest Christianity.* Grand Rapids, Mich.: Eerdmans, 2003.

Isaac, E. "1 (Ethiopic Apocalypse of) ENOCH." In *The Old Testament Pseudepigrapha,* vol. 1, ed. James H. Charlesworth, 5–89. New York: Doubleday, 1983.

Johnson, Luke T. "The New Testament's Anti-Jewish Slander and the Conventions of Ancient Polemic." *JBL* 108 (1989): 419–41.

Johnson, Marshall D. "Reflections on a Wisdom Approach to Matthew's Christology." *CBQ* 36 (1974): 44–64.

Jonge, Marinus de. "Monotheism and Christology." In *Early Christian Thought in its Jewish Context,* ed. John Barclay and John Sweet, 225–37. Cambridge: Cambridge University Press, 1996.

————. *God's Final Envoy.* Grand Rapids, Mich.: Eerdmans, 1998.

Kanagaraj, Jeyaseelan Joseph. *"Mysticism" in the Gospel of John: An Inquiry into Its Background.* Journal for the Study of the New Testament, Supplement Series 158. Sheffield, UK: Sheffield Academic, 1998.

Katz, Steven T. "Issues in the Separation of Judaism and Christianity After 70 C.E.: A Reconsideration." *JBL* 103, no. 1 (1984): 43–76.

Kee, Howard Clark. *The Beginnings of Christianity.* New York: T&T Clark, 2005.

Kimelman, Reuven. "Birkat Ha-Minim and the Lack of Evidence for an Anti-Christian Jewish Prayer in Late Antiquity." In *Jewish and Christian Self-Definition.* Vol. 2, *Aspects of Judaism in the Graeco-Roman Period,* ed. E. P. Sanders, A. I. Baumgarten, and Alan Mendelson, 226–44. London: SCM Press, 1981.

Klausner, Joseph. *The Messianic Idea in Israel from Its Beginning to the Completion of the Mishnah.* London: George Allen and Unwin, 1956.

Kreitzer, Larry J. *Jesus and God in Paul's Eschatology.* Journal for the Study of the New Testament, Supplement Series 19. Sheffield, UK: Sheffield Academic, 1987.

Kysar, Robert. "Christology and Controversy: The Contributions of the Prologue of the Gospel of John to New Testament Christology and their Historical Setting." *CTM* 5 (1978): 348–64.

Laato, Antti. *Monotheism, the Trinity, and Mysticism: A Semiotic Approach to Jewish-Christian Encounter.* New York: Peter Lang, 1999.

Lang, Bernard. *Sacred Games: A History of Christian Worship.* New Haven, Conn.: Yale University Press, 1997.

Levison, John R. *Portraits of Adam in Early Judaism: From Sirach to 2 Baruch.* Journal for the Study of the Pseudepigrapha Supplement 1. Sheffield, UK: JSOT/Sheffield Academic, 1988.

Lieu, Judith. *The Theology of the Johannine Epistles.* New Testament Theology Series. Cambridge: Cambridge University Press, 1991.

Lindars, Barnabas. *The Gospel of John.* Grand Rapids, Mich.: Eerdmans; London: Marshall, Morgan and Scott, 1972.

Loader, William R. G. *The Christology of the Fourth Gospel: Structure and Issues.* 2nd ed. BBET 23. Frankfurt: Peter Lang, 1992.

Louth, Andrew. *The Origins of the Christian Mystical Tradition: From Plato to Denys.* Oxford: Clarendon Press, 1981.

Mach, Michael. *Entwicklungsstadien des jüdischen Engelglaubens in vorrabbinischer Zeit.* Texte und Studien zum Antiken Judentum 34. Tübingen: Mohr-Siebeck, 1992.

Malina, Bruce J. *The New Testament World: Insights from Cultural Anthropology.* Atlanta: John Knox Press, 1981.

———. *Windows on the World of Jesus: Time Travel to Ancient Judea.* Louisville, Ky.: Westminster John Knox Press, 1993.

Manns, Frédéric. *John and Jamnia: How the Break Occurred Between Jews and Christians, c. 80–100 A.D.* Jerusalem: Franciscan Printing Press, 1988.

———. *L'Evangile de Jean à la lumière du Judaisme.* Studium Biblicum Franciscanum Analecta 33. Jerusalem: Franciscan Printing Press, 1991.

Marcus, Joel. *The Way of the Lord: Christological Exegesis of the Old Testament in the Gospel of Mark.* Louisville, Ky.: Westminster John Knox; Edinburgh: T&T Clark, 1992.

Marshall, I. Howard. "The Development of Christology in the Early Church." *Tyndale Bulletin* 18 (1967): 77–93.

———. *The Origins of New Testament Christology.* Updated ed. Leicester, UK: Apollos/Inter-Varsity Press, 1990.

Martin, Ralph P., and Brian J. Dodd, eds. *Where Christology Began: Essays on Philippians 2.* Louisville: Westminster John Knox, 1998.

Martyn, J. Louis. "Glimpses into the History of the Johannine Community." In *L'Évangile de Jean: Sources, rédaction, théologie,* ed. M. de Jonge, 149–75. BETL 44. Leuven: Leuven University Press, 1977.

———. *History and Theology in the Fourth Gospel.* 2nd ed. Nashville: Abingdon, 1979.

———. "A Gentile Mission that Replaced an Earlier Jewish Mission?" In *Exploring the Gospel of John: In Honor of D. Moody Smith,* ed. R. Alan Culpepper and C. Clifton Black, 124–44. Louisville, Ky.: Westminster John Knox, 1996.

Mastin, B. A. "A Neglected Feature of the Christology of the Fourth Gospel." *NTS* 22 (1975): 32–51.

Matsunaga, Kikuo. "The 'Theos' Christology as the Ultimate Confession of the Fourth Gospel." In *Annual of the Japanese Biblical Institute*, vol. 7, ed. Masao Sekine and Akira Satake, 124–45. Tokyo: Yamamoto Shoten, 1981.

Mauser, Ulrich W. "Εἰς Θεος und Μονος Θεος in Biblischer Theologie." *Jahrbuch für biblische Theologie* 1 (1986): 71–87.

———. "One God Alone: A Pillar of Biblical Theology." *PSB* 12 (1991): 255–65.

May, Gerhard. *Creatio ex Nihilo: The Doctrine of "Creation out of Nothing" in Early Christian Thought*. Edinburgh: T&T Clark, 1994.

McEleney, Neil J. "Orthodoxy in Judaism of the First Christian Century: Replies to David E. Aune and Lester L. Grabbe." *JSJ* 9, no. 1 (1978): 83–88.

McGrath, James F. "Johannine Christianity—Jewish Christianity?" *Koinonia Journal* 8, no. 1 (1996): 1–20.

———. "Going Up and Coming Down in Johannine Legitimation." *Neotestamentica* 31, no. 1 (1997): 107–18.

———. "Prologue as Legitimation: Christological Controversy and the Interpretation of John 1:1–18." *IBS* 19 (1997): 98–120.

———. "Uncontrived Messiah or Passover Plot? A Study of a Johannine Apologetic Motif." *IBS* 19 (1997): 2–16.

———. "Change in Christology: New Testament Models and the Contemporary Task." *ITQ* 63, no. 1 (1998): 39–50.

———. "A Rebellious Son? Hugo Odeberg and the Interpretation of John 5.18." *NTS* 44 (1998): 470–73.

———. "Christology on Two Fronts: A New Testament Model for Doing Christology in a Pluralistic Context." *Religion and Theology* 6, no. 1 (1999): 65–82.

———. *John's Apologetic Christology*. Society for New Testament Studies, Monograph Series 111. Cambridge: Cambridge University Press, 2001.

McGrath, James F., and Jerry Truex. "'Two Powers' and Early Jewish and Christian Monotheism." *JBS* 4, no. 1 (January 2004): 43–71.

McReynolds, Paul R. "John 1:18 in Textual Variation and Translation." In *New Testament Criticism: Its Significance for Exegesis. Essays in Honour of Bruce M. Metzger*, ed. Eldon Jay Epp and Gordon D. Fee, 105–30. Oxford: Clarendon Press, 1981.

Mealand, David L. "The Christology of the Fourth Gospel." *SJT* 31 (1978): 449–67.

Meeks, Wayne A. *The Prophet-King: Moses Traditions and the Johannine Christology*. NovTSup 14. Leiden: E. J. Brill, 1967.

———. "Moses as God and King." In *Religions in Antiquity: Essays in Memory of E. R. Goodenough*, ed. Jacob Neusner, 354–71. Numen Supplement 14. Leiden: E. J. Brill, 1968.

———. "'Am I A Jew?' Johannine Christianity and Judaism." In *Christianity, Judaism and Other Greco-Roman Cults: Studies for Morton Smith at Sixty*. Pt. 1, *New Testament*, ed. Jacob Neusner, 163–86. *SJLA* 12. Leiden: E. J. Brill, 1975.

———. "The Divine Agent and His Counterfeit in Philo and the Fourth Gospel." In *Aspects of Religious Propaganda in Judaism and Early Christianity*, ed. Elizabeth Schüssler Fiorenza, 43–67. Notre Dame, Ind.: University of Notre Dame Press, 1976.

———. "Breaking Away: Three New Testament Pictures of Christianity's Separation from the Jewish Communities." In *"To See Ourselves as Others See Us": Christians, Jews, "Others" in Late Antiquity*, ed. Jacob Neusner and Ernest S. Frerichs, 93–115. Chico, Calif.: Scholars Press, 1985.

———. "The Man from Heaven in Johannine Sectarianism." In *The Interpretation of John*, ed. John Ashton, 141–73. Issues in Religion and Theology 9. Philadelphia: Fortress Press; London: SPCK, 1986.

———. "Equal to God." In *The Conversation Continues: Studies in Paul and John in Honor of J. Louis Martyn*, ed. Robert T. Fortna and Beverly R. Gaventa, 309–21. Nashville: Abingdon Press, 1990.

Menken, Maarten J. J. "The Christology of the Fourth Gospel: A Survey of Recent Research." In *From Jesus to John: Essays on Jesus and New Testament Christology in Honour of Marinus de Jonge*, ed. Martinus C. de Boer, 292–320. Journal for the Study of the New Testament, Supplement Series 84. Sheffield, UK: Sheffield Academic, 1993.

———. *Old Testament Quotations in the Fourth Gospel: Studies in Textual Form*. Contributions to Biblical Exegesis and Theology 15. Kampen, Netherlands: Kok Pharos, 1996.

———. "The Use of the Septuagint in Three Quotations in John: Jn 10, 34; 12, 38; 19, 24." In *The Scriptures in the Gospels*, ed. Christopher M. Tuckett, 367–93. BETL 131. Leuven: Leuven University Press, 1997.

Mercer, Calvin. "Jesus the Apostle: 'Sending' and the Theology of John." *JETS* 35, no. 4 (December 1992): 457–62.

Merrigan, Terrence, and Jacques Haers, eds. *The Myriad Christ: Plurality and the Quest for Unity in Contemporary Christology*. BETL 152. Leuven: Peeters, 2000.

Metzger, Bruce M. "The Punctuation of Rom. 9:5." In *Christ and Spirit in the New Testament*, ed. Barnabas Lindars and Stephen S. Smalley, 95–112. Cambridge: Cambridge University Press, 1973.

Meyer, Paul W. "'The Father': The Presentation of God in the Fourth Gospel." In *Exploring the Gospel of John in Honor of D. Moody Smith*, ed. R. Alan Culpepper and C. Clifton Black, 255–73. Louisville, Ky.: Westminster John Knox, 1996.

Minear, Paul S. "Diversity and Unity: A Johannine Case Study." In *Die Mitte des Neuen Testaments: Einheit und Vielfalt neutestamentlicher Theologie: Festschrift für Eduard Schweizer zum siebzigsten Geburtstag*, ed. Ulrich Luz and Hans Weder, 162–75. Göttingen: Vandenhoeck and Ruprecht, 1983.

———. "Logos Affiliations in Johannine Thought." In *Christology in Dialogue*, ed. Robert F. Berkey and Sarah A. Edwards, 142–56. Cleveland: Pilgrim Press, 1993.

Mitchell, Margaret M. "New Testament Envoys in the Context of Greco-Roman Diplomatic and Epistolary Conventions: The Example of Timothy and Titus." *JBL* 111, no. 4 (1992): 641–62.

Moeller, Henry R. "Wisdom Motifs in John's Gospel." *Bulletin of the Evangelical Theological Society* 6 (1963): 92–100.

Moloney, Francis J. "The Fourth Gospel's Presentation of Jesus as 'The Christ' and J. A. T. Robinson's Redating." *Downside Review* 95 (1977): 239–53.

Moore, George Foot. *Judaism in the First Centuries of the Christian Era: The Age of the Tannaim*, vol. 1. Cambridge: Harvard University Press, 1927.

Morgan-Wynne, J. E. "The Cross and the Revelation of Jesus as εγω ειμι in the Fourth Gospel." In *Studia Biblica 1978*. Vol. 2, *Papers on the Gospels: Sixth International Congress on Biblical Studies, Oxford 3–7 April 1978*, ed. E. A. Livingstone, 219–26. Journal for the Study of the New Testament, Supplement Series 2. Sheffield, UK: JSOT/Sheffield Academic, 1980.

Morwood, Michael. *Is Jesus God? Finding Our Faith*. New York: Crossroad, 2001.

Moule, C. F. D. *The Origin of Christology*. Cambridge: Cambridge University Press, 1977.

Moxnes, Halvor. *Theology in Conflict: Studies in Paul's Understanding of God in Romans*. NovTSup 53. Leiden: Brill, 1980.

Newman, Carey C., James S. Davila, and Gladys S. Lewis, eds. *The Jewish Roots of Christological Monotheism*. Supplements to the Journal for the Study of Judaism 63. Leiden: Brill, 1999.

Neyrey, Jerome. *Christ Is Community: The Christologies of the New Testament*. Good News Studies 13. Wilmington, Del.: Michael Glazier, 1985.

———. "'My Lord and My God': The Divinity of Jesus in John's Gospel." *Society of Biblical Literature 1986 Seminar Papers*, ed. K. H. Richards, 152–71. Atlanta: Scholars Press, 1986.

———. *An Ideology of Revolt: John's Christology in Social-Science Perspective*. Philadelphia: Fortress Press, 1988.

———. "'I Said: You are Gods': Psalm 82:6 and John 10." *JBL* 108, no. 4 (1989): 647–63.

Nilsson, Martin P. "The High God and the Mediator." *HTR* 56, no. 2 (1963): 101–20.

O'Brien, Peter T. *Colossians, Philemon*. Word Biblical Commentary 44. Dallas: Word, 1982.

Ohlig, Karl-Heinz. *One or Three? From the Father of Jesus to the Trinity*. Saarbrücker Theologische Forschungen 8. Frankfurt: Peter Lang, 2002.

Olsson, Birger. "*Deus Semper Maior?* On God in the Johannine Writings." In *New Readings in John: Literary and Theological Perspectives*, ed. Johannes Nissen and Sigfred Pedersen, 143–71. Journal for the Study of the New Testament, Supplement Series 182. Sheffield, UK: Sheffield Academic, 1999.

O'Neill, John. *Who Did Jesus Think He Was?* Leiden: Brill, 1996.

Osborn, Eric. *The Emergence of Christian Theology*. Cambridge: Cambridge University Press, 1993.

Pagels, Elaine. *The Gnostic Gospels*. London: Penguin, 1979.

Painter, John. "Christology and the History of the Johannine Community in the Prologue of the Fourth Gospel." *NTS* 30 (1984): 460–74.

Pamment, Margaret. "Is There Convincing Evidence of Samaritan Influence on the Fourth Gospel?" *ZNW* 73 (1982): 221–30.

Pancaro, Severino. *The Law in the Fourth Gospel: The Torah and the Gospel, Moses and Jesus, Judaism and Christianity according to John*. NovTSup 42. Leiden: E. J. Brill, 1975.

Peterson, Erik. ΕΙΣ ΘΕΟΣ. *Epigraphische, formgeschichtliche und religionsgeschichtliche Untersuchungen*. FRLANT, n.s., 24. Göttingen: Vandenhoeck & Ruprecht, 1926.

Porter, Andrew P. *Elementary Monotheism*, vols. 1 and 2. Lanham, Md.: University Press of America, 2001.

Prestige, G. L. *God in Patristic Thought.* London: SPCK, 1952.

Rainbow, Paul A. "Monotheism and Christology in 1 Corinthians 8:4–6." D.Phil. diss., Oxford University, 1988.

———. "Jewish Monotheism as the Matrix for New Testament Christology: A Review Article." *NovT* 33, no. 1 (1991): 78–91.

Reim, Günter. "Jesus as God in the Fourth Gospel: The Old Testament Background." *NTS* 30 (1984): 158–60.

Rensberger, David. *Overcoming the World: Politics and Community in the Gospel of John.* London: SPCK, 1989. First published as *Johannine Faith and Liberating Community.* Philadelphia: Westminster Press, 1988.

Richardson, Neil. *Paul's Language About God.* Journal for the Study of the New Testament, Supplement Series 99. Sheffield, UK: Sheffield Academic, 1994.

Riches, John K. *Jesus and the Transformation of Judaism.* New York: Seabury, 1980.

Robinson, John A. T. *The Priority of John.* London: SCM Press, 1985.

Rosenbaum, Stanley Ned. *Understanding Biblical Israel: A Reexamination of the Origins of Monotheism.* Macon, Ga.: Mercer University Press, 2002.

Roth, Wolfgang. "Jesus as the Son of Man: The Scriptural Identity of a Johannine Image." In *The Living Text: Essays in Honor of Ernest W. Saunders,* ed. Dennis E. Groh and Robert Jewett, 11–26. Lanham, Md.: University Press of America, 1985.

Rowdon, Harold H., ed. *Christ the Lord: Studies in Christology presented to Donald Guthrie.* Leicester, UK: Inter-Varsity Press, 1982.

Rowland, Christopher. *The Open Heaven: A Study of Apocalyptic in Judaism and Early Christianity.* London: SPCK, 1982.

———. *Christian Origins: An Account of the Setting and Character of the Most Important Messianic Sect of Judaism.* London: SPCK, 1985.

Sanders, E. P. "Testament of Abraham." In *The Old Testament Pseudepigrapha.* Vol. 1, *Apocalyptic Literature and Testaments,* ed. James H. Charlesworth, 871–902. New York: Doubleday, 1983.

———. *Judaism: Practice and Belief, 63 BCE–66 CE.* London: SCM Press; Philadelphia: Trinity Press International, 1992.

Sanders, Jack T. *Schismatics, Sectarians, Dissidents, Deviants: The First One Hundred Years of Jewish-Christian Relations.* London: SCM Press, 1993.

Sanders, J. N. *The Fourth Gospel in the Early Church: Its Origin and Influence on Christian Theology up to Irenaeus.* Cambridge: Cambridge University Press, 1943.

Sanders, J. N. Completed and edited by B. A. Mastin. *The Gospel According to St. John.* London: A. & C. Black, 1968.

Schäfer, Peter. "The Jewish God." In *Judeophobia: Attitudes Toward the Jews in the Ancient World,* by Peter Schäfer, 34–65. Cambridge: Harvard University Press, 1997.

Schelkle, Karl Hermann. "Jesus—Lehrer und Prophet." In *Orientierung an Jesus: Zur Theologie der Synoptiker: Für Josef Schmid,* ed. Paul Hoffmann, N. Brox, and W. Pesch, 300–308. Freiburg: Herder, 1973.

Schimanowski, Gottfried. *Weisheit und Messias: Die jüdischen Voraussetzungen der urchristlichen Präexistenzchristologie.* WUNT 2:17. Tübingen: J. C. B. Mohr (Paul Siebeck), 1985.

Schnackenburg, Rudolf. "Synoptische und Johanneische Christologie: Ein Vergleich." In *The Four Gospels 1992: Festschrift Frans Neirynck*, vol. 3, ed. F. van Segbroeck, C. M. Tuckett, G. van Belle, and J. Verheyden, 1723–50. BETL 100. Leuven: Leuven University Press, 1992.

Schnelle, Udo. *Antidocetic Christology in the Gospel of John: An Investigation of the Place of the Fourth Gospel in the Johannine School*. Minneapolis: Fortress Press, 1992.

Schnider, Franz. *Jesus der Prophet*. Orbis Biblicus et Orientalis 2. Freiburg: Universitätsverlag Freiburg (Schweiz); Göttingen: Vandenhoeck & Ruprecht, 1973.

Schoonenberg, Piet. "A Sapiential Reading of John's Prologue: Some Reflection on Views of Reginald Fuller and James Dunn." *Theology Digest* 33, no. 4 (1986): 403–21.

Schuchard, Bruce G. *Scripture Within Scripture: The Interrelationship of Form and Function in the Explicit Old Testament Citations in the Gospel of John*. SBL Dissertation Series 133. Atlanta: Scholars Press, 1992.

Scott, Martin. *Sophia and the Johannine Jesus*. Journal for the Study of the New Testament, Supplement Series 71. Sheffield, UK: Sheffield Academic, 1992.

Scroggs, Robin. *The Last Adam: A Study in Pauline Anthropology*. Philadelphia: Fortress Press; Oxford: Basil Blackwell, 1966.

———. *Christology in Paul and John: The Reality and Revelation of God*. Proclamation Commentaries. Philadelphia: Fortress Press, 1988.

Segal, Alan F. *Two Powers in Heaven: Early Rabbinic Reports about Christianity and Gnosticism*. SJLA 25. Leiden: E. J. Brill, 1977.

———. "Ruler of this World: Attitudes about Mediator Figures and the Importance of Sociology for Self-Definition." In *Jewish and Christian Self-Definition*. Volume 2, *Aspects of Judaism in the Graeco-Roman Period*, ed. E. P. Sanders, A. I. Baumgarten and Alan Mendelson, 245–68. London: SCM Press, 1981.

———. *Rebecca's Children: Judaism and Christianity in the Roman World*. Cambridge: Harvard University Press, 1986.

———. *The Other Judaisms of Late Antiquity*. Brown Judaic Studies 127. Atlanta: Scholars Press, 1987.

———. "Outlining the Question: From Christ to God." In *Jews and Christians Speak of Jesus*, ed. Arthur E. Zannoni, 125–35. Minneapolis: Fortress Press, 1994.

Setzer, Claudia J. *Jewish Responses to Early Christians: History and Polemics, 30–150 C.E.* Minneapolis: Fortress Press, 1994.

Shutt, R. J. H. "The Concept of God in the Works of Flavius Josephus." *JJS* 31 (1980): 171–87.

Skarsaune, Oskar. "Is Christianity Monotheistic? Patristic Perspectives on a Jewish-Christian Debate." *Studia Patristica* 29 (1997): 340–63.

Smiga, George M. *Pain and Polemic: Anti-Judaism in the Gospels*. Mahwah, N.J.: Paulist Press, 1992.

Smith, J. Z. "The Prayer of Joseph." In *Religions in Antiquity: Essays in Memory of E. R. Goodenough*, ed. Jacob Neusner, 253–94. Numen Supplement 14. Leiden: E. J. Brill, 1968.

———. "Fences and Neighbours: Some Contours of Early Judaism." In *Approaches to Ancient Judaism*, vol. 2, ed. William Scott Green, 1–25. Brown Judaic Studies 9. Chico, Calif.: Scholars Press, 1980.

———. "Prayer of Joseph: A New Translation with Introduction." In *The Old Testament Pseudepigrapha*, vol. 2, ed. James H. Charlesworth, 699–714. Garden City, N.Y.: Doubleday, 1985.

Smith, Morton. "Ascent to the Heavens and the Beginnings of Christianity." *Eranos* 50 (1981): 403–29.

———. "Two Ascended to Heaven—Jesus and the Author of 4Q491." In *Jesus and the Dead Sea Scrolls*, ed. James H. Charlesworth, 290–301. New York: Doubleday, 1992.

Stanton, Graham. "Samaritan Incarnational Christology?" In *Incarnation and Myth: The Debate Continued*, ed. Michael Goulder, 243–46. London: SCM, 1979.

Steenburg, D. "The Worship of Adam and Christ as the Image of God." *Journal for the Study of the New Testament* 39 (1990): 95–109.

Stemberger, Günter. *Introduction to the Talmud and Midrash*. 2nd ed. Edinburgh: T&T Clark, 1996.

Stolz, Fritz. *Einfuhrung in den biblischen Monotheismus*. Darmstadt: Wissenschaftliche Buchgesellschaft, 1996.

Stuckenbruck, Loren T. "An Angelic Refusal of Worship: The Tradition and Its Function in the Apocalypse of John." In *Society of Biblical Literature 1994 Seminar Papers*, ed. Eugene Lovelace, 679–96. Atlanta: Scholars Press, 1994.

———. *Angel Veneration and Christology: A Study in Early Judaism and in the Christology of the Apocalypse of John*. WUNT 2:70. Tübingen: J. C. B. Mohr (Paul Siebeck), 1995.

———. "'One Like a Son of Man as the Ancient of Days' in the Old Greek Recension of Daniel 7,13: Scribal Error or Theological Translation?" *ZNW* 86 (1995): 268–76.

Stuckenbruck, Loren T., and Wendy E. S. North, eds. *Early Jewish and Christian Monotheism*. Journal for the Study of the New Testament, Supplement Series 263. New York: Continuum, 2004.

Suggs, M. Jack. *Wisdom, Christology and Law in Matthew's Gospel*. Cambridge: Harvard University Press, 1970.

Sundberg, Albert C. "*Isos to Theo*: Christology in John 5.17–30." *BR* 15 (1970): 19–31.

Talbert, Charles H. *Reading John: A Literary and Theological Commentary on the Fourth Gospel and the Johannine Epistles*. London: SPCK, 1992.

———. "'And the Word Became Flesh': When?" In *The Future of Christology: Essays in Honor of Leander E. Keck*, ed. Abraham J. Malherbe and Wayne A. Meeks, 43–52. Minneapolis: Fortress Press, 1993.

Taylor, Miriam S. *Anti-Judaism and Early Christian Identity: A Critique of Scholarly Consensus*. Studia Post-Biblica 46. Leiden: E. J. Brill, 1995.

Theobald, Michael. *Die Fleischwerdung des Logos: Studien zum Verhältnis des Johannesprologs zum Corpus des Evangeliums und zu 1 Joh*. Neutestamentliche Abhandlungen 20. Muenster: Aschendorffsche Verlagsbuchhandlung, 1988.

———. "Gott, Logos und Pneuma: 'Trinitarische' Rede von Gott im Johannesevangelium." In *Monotheismus und Christologie: Zur Gottesfrage im Hellenistischen Judentum und im Urchristentum*, ed. Hans-Josef Klauck, 41–87. Quaestiones Disputatae 138. Freiburg: Herder, 1992.

Thoma, Clemens, and Michael Wyschogrod, eds. *Das Reden vom einen Gott bei Juden und Christen*. Bern: Peter Lang, 1984.

Thompson, Marianne Meye. *The Humanity of Jesus in the Fourth Gospel*. Philadelphia: Fortress Press, 1988.

———. "John, Gospel of." In *Dictionary of Jesus and the Gospels*, ed. Joel B. Green, Scot McKnight, and I. Howard Marshall, 368–83. Leicester: InterVarsity Press, 1992.

———. *The God of the Gospel of John*. Grand Rapids, Mich.: Eerdmans, 2001.

Twelftree, Graham H. "Blasphemy." In *Dictionary of Jesus and the Gospels*, ed. Joel B. Green, Scot McKnight, and I. Howard Marshall, 75–77. Leicester: InterVarsity Press, 1992.

Urbach, Ephraim E. "The Belief in One God." In *The Sages: The World and Wisdom of the Rabbis of the Talmud*, by Ephraim E. Urbach. Cambridge: Harvard University Press, 1987.

Van der Horst, Pieter W. "Moses' Throne Vision in Ezekiel the Dramatist." *JJS* 34 (1983): 21–29.

VanderKam, James C. "John 10 and the Feast of Dedication." In *Of Scribes and Scrolls: Studies on the Hebrew Bible, Intertestamental Judaism, and Christian Origins Presented to John Strugnell on the Occasion of His Sixtieth Birthday*, ed. H. W. Attridge, J. J. Collins, and T. H. Tobin, 203–14. College Theology Society Resources in Religion 5. Lanham, Md.: University Press of America, 1990.

Vermes, Geza. *Jesus the Jew: A Historian's Reading of the Gospels*. London: Fontana/Collins, 1973.

Vogel, Manfred H. "Monotheism." In *Encyclopaedia Judaica*, vol. 12, cols. 260–63. Jerusalem: Keter, 1971.

Watson, Francis. "Is John's Christology Adoptionist?" In *The Glory of Christ in the New Testament: Studies in Christology in Memory of G. B. Caird*, ed. L. D. Hurst and N. T. Wright, 113–24. Oxford: Clarendon Press, 1987.

Wedderburn, A. J. M. "Adam in Paul's Letter to the Romans." In *Studia Biblica 1978*, vol. 3, ed. E. A. Livingstone, 413–30. Journal for the Study of the New Testament, Supplement Series 3. Sheffield, UK: Sheffield Academic, 1978.

Whitacre, Rodney. *Johannine Polemic: The Role of Tradition and Theology*. SBL Dissertation Series 67. Chico, Calif.: Scholars Press, 1982.

Wicks, Henry J. *The Doctrine of God in the Jewish Apocryphal and Apocalyptic Literature*. New York: KTAV, 1971.

Wiles, Maurice. *The Making of Christian Doctrine: A Study in the Principles of Early Christian Doctrinal Development*. Cambridge: Cambridge University Press, 1967.

———. "Person or Personification? A Patristic Debate about Logos." In *The Glory of Christ in the New Testament*, ed. L. D. Hurst and N. T. Wright, 281–89. Oxford: Clarendon Press, 1987.

Willett, Michael E. *Wisdom Christology in the Fourth Gospel*. San Francisco: Mellen Research University Press, 1992.

Williams, Catrin H. *I am He: The Interpretation of* Anî Hû *in Jewish and Early Christian Literature*. Tübingen: Mohr-Siebeck, 2000.

Wilson, R. McL. *The Gnostic Problem: A Study of the Relations between Hellenistic Judaism and the Gnostic Heresy*. London: A. R. Mowbray, 1958.

Witherington, Ben, III. *The Christology of Jesus*. Minneapolis: Fortress Press, 1990.

————. *Jesus the Sage*. Minneapolis: Fortress Press; Edinburgh: T&T Clark, 1994.

————. *Paul's Narrative Thought World*. Louisville, Ky.: Westminster John Knox, 1994.

————. *John's Wisdom: A Commentary on the Fourth Gospel*. Louisville, Ky.: Westminster John Knox, 1995.

Wright, N. T. *The Climax of the Covenant: Christ and the Law in Pauline Theology*. Edinburgh: T&T Clark, 1991.

————. *Christian Origins and the Question of God*. Vol. 1, *The New Testament and the People of God*. London: SPCK, 1992.

————. *Paul in Fresh Perspective*. Minneapolis: Fortress Press, 2005.

INDEX OF MODERN AUTHORS

INDEX OF SUBJECTS

INDEX OF ANCIENT SOURCES

JAMES F. MCGRATH is associate professor of religion at Butler University in Indianapolis, Indiana. He is the author of *John's Apologetic Christology* and *The Burial of Jesus: History and Faith*, as well as a number of academic articles and book chapters related to the Gospel of John, the Christology of the earliest Christians, ancient Jewish and Christian monotheism, the historical figure of Jesus, and religion and science fiction. He also maintains a blog, Exploring Our Matrix, where he ponders these and other subjects that interest him on a regular basis.